The Chindali Language of Malawi
Volume 2

A Grammatical Sketch of Chindali
(Malawian variety)

Robert Botne

American Philosophical Society
Philadelphia • 2008

Lightning Rod Press
American Philosophical Society
Held at Philadelphia For Promoting Useful Knowledge
Number 2

ISBN 978-1-60618-911-5

Library of Congress Cataloging-in-Publication Data

Botne, Robert Dale Olson, 1950-
The Chindali language of Malawi / compiled by Robert Botne, in collaboration with
Loveness Schafer.
    p. cm. — (Lightning rod press series ; 1-3)
    Includes bibliographical references and index.
    ISBN 978-1-60618-911-5
    1. Ndali language—Dictionaries—English. 2. English language—Dictionaries—
Ndali. 3. Ndali language—Grammar. 4. Malawi—Social life and customs.
I. Schafer, Loveness, 1965- II. Title.

PL8547.N26B68 2008
496'.393—dc22   2008035129

Cover Design and Editorial by Inornational Graphic Services.

Printed by Diane Publishing Company.

CONTENTS

ACKNOWLEDGMENTS

This sketch of aspects of Chindali grammar grew out of work originally begun in a Field Methods class at Indiana University in 1995. The primary consultant for both that class and later work has been Loveness Schafer, whom I deeply thank for her endless patience in working through and editing the Chindali data. I also wish to express thanks to many other Chindali speakers who contributed, either directly or indirectly, to this effort, more than thirty of whom contributed a variety of texts that have provided valuable data on use of the language in narrative discourse. This work would not have been possible without their contributions. Finally, I thank Pamela Lankas for her assiduous attention in editing the manuscript.

I wish, as well, to express thanks to Indiana University for its support of the primary language consultant, via the Field Methods class. In addition, I acknowledge further institutional support that allowed me to complete this sketch on a sabbatical leave in fall 2004.

NOTE

The use of British punctuation in this volume follows the style preferred by the author.

ABBREVIATIONS

ADJ	adjective		O	onset
ADV	adverb		OM	object marker
AGR	agreement		OO	oblique object
ANT	anterior		P	plural
APP	applicative		PASS	passive
ASP	aspect		Pfx	prefix
C	consonant [phonology]		PL	plural
	coda [event structure]		PO	primary object
CAUS	causative		PoF	post-final clitic
CO	coincident		POSS	possessive
CL	noun class		POT	potential
CMPL	completive		PRCL	pro-clitic
COP	copula		RAD	radical
EFF	efferential		REC	reciprocal
e. o.	each other		REL	relative marker
Ext	extension		RM	remote past
F	verb final suffix		S	singular [morphology]
FUT	future			speech time [tense
G	glide			schemas]
H	high tone		SG	singular
IMPF	imperfective		SO	secondary object
INF	infinitive		s.o.	someone
IT	itive		SP	subject prefix
LNK	linker		sth.	something
LIT	literal(ly)		SUBJ	subjunctive
LOC	locative		SVO	subject-verb-object
M	mood		Vox	voice changing suffix
N	nasal consonant [phonology]		T	tense
	noun [morphology]		Ten	tenor
	nucleus [event structure]		TMP	tempus marking
NC	nasal + consonant cluster		V	vowel [phonological]
NEG	negative			verb [verbal construction]
NPfx	noun class prefix		V_S	stem vowel

xiii

Numbers unaccompanied by an S or P in a gloss refer to the class of the noun, following the conventional practice of numbering Bantu noun classes.

A contrast between plain and bold text in verb templates highlights (1) obligatory vs optional grammatical affixes, or, in a few cases, (2) the relevant grammatical markers in that construction.

INTRODUCTION

Chindali—*Ichííndali* in the language itself—is spoken along the northern border of Malawi and in southwestern Tanzania (see map on following page). There are approximately 70,000 speakers—*abáándali* (singular *umúúndali*)— in Malawi and 150,000 speakers in Tanzania ((Gordon 2005, citing a 2003 source and a 1987 source, respectively). It is classified as M.21 in the Tervuren (Bastin 1978) revison of Guthrie's (1967-70) zone classification.

This grammatical sketch represents the language as spoken in the region of northern Malawi. It differs in important ways from the variety spoken in Tanzania, especially in verbal morphology. It also differs from a closely related dialect called Chisukwa, primarily in tone and some sounds, as well as with some verbal conjugations. The Ndali people live in close proximity to the Sukwa people.

Chindali is agglutinating, like most Bantu languages, with a basic SVO word order. The sketch describes the principal features of the language.

Data for the study have come from Loveness Shafer, the primary language consultant, and from approximately 45+ texts collected in written form by Loveness Shafer from approximately 30 speakers in 1995.

• Orthography and orthographic conventions

There is no standard orthography for Chindali, although there is for Chichewa, a national language of Malawi. Several competing orthographies were created. For this sketch, a broad phonetic transcription has been employed for vowel quality—a, e, i, o, ,u—and for most consonants. The following orthography, then, has been adopted: a, b, ch, d, e, f, g, h, i, j, k, l, m, n, ng', ny', o, p, r, s, t u, w, y, z. Some of these symbols are necessary for sound contrasts specific to Chindali and do not always have the more conventional association:

b	=	[ʋ]	ny	=	[nʸ]
ch	=	[tʃ]	ny'	=	[ɲ]
g	=	[ɣ]	ng	=	[ŋg]
j	=	[dʒ] or [ʒ]	ng'	=	[ŋ]

The symbol [ʋ] represents a bilabial sound that seems intermediate be-tween a fricative and glide. Similarly, [ɣ] is a velar with very light frication.

Vowel length is contrastive and is indicated by a sequence of two vowels, e.g., *uku.baala* 'to increase' in contrast with *uku.bala* 'to shine', *ichi.liilo* 'burden' in contrast with *ichi.lilo* 'mourning', and *-kuulu* 'old' in contrast with *-kulu* 'big'.

1

Map: Approximate location of Chindali

Lake Rukwa

TANZANIA

CHINDALI

ZAMBIA

Lake
Nyasa

MOZAMBIQUE

MALAWI

BIBLIOGRAPHIC RESOURCES ON CHINDALI AND CHISUKWA

Chindali

Berger, Paul. 1934-35. 'Ndali-Texte.' *Zeitschrift für Eingeborenen-Spra-chen* 25: 229-239, 284-307.

Berger, Paul. 1937-38. 'Die mit B. -île gebildeten Perfektstämme in den Bantusprachen.' *Zeitschrift für Eingeborenen-Sprachen* 28: 81-286. [Chindali pp. 91-96, 275-78]

Botne, Robert. 1998. 'Prosodically-conditioned vowel shortening in Chindali.' *Studies in African Lingustics* 27, 1: 97-121.

Botne, Robert. 2003. 'Dissociation in tense, realis, and location in Chindali verbs.' *Anthropological Linguistics* 45, 4: 390-412.

Botne, Robert. 2005. 'Cognitive schemas and motion verbs: Coming and Going in Chindali.' *Cognitive Linguistics* 16, 1: 43-80.

Botne, Robert. 2008. *A Chindali and English Dictionary.* Philadelphia: American Philosophical Society.

Botne, Robert Botne. 2008. *Narratives of Ndali life and culture.* Philadelphia: American Philosophical Society.

Kishindo, Pascal J. 1998. 'Diminution, augmentation and pejorativeness in Icindali: The semantics of classes 5/6, 3/4, 7/8 and 21.' *Journal of the Humanities* (Zomba, Malawi) 12: 44-55.

Swilla, Imani N. 1981. 'The noun class system and agreement in Chindali.' In *La civilisation ancienne des peuples des grands lacs*, Centre de la Civilisation Burundaise. Paris: Éditions Karthala. Pp. 379-393.

Swilla, Imani N. 1998. 'Tenses in Chindali.' *Afrikanistische Arbeits-papiere* 54:95-125.

Swilla, Imani N. 2000. 'Borrowing in Chindali.' In *Lugha za Tanzania/ Languages of Tanzania*, Kulikoyela Kahigi, Yared Kihore, and Maarten Mous (eds.). CNWS: Universiteit Leiden. Pp. 297-307.

Swilla, Imani N. 2000. 'Names in Chindali.' *Afrikanistische Arbeitspapiere* 63: 35-62.

3

Vail, Leroy. 1974. 'The noun classes of Ndali.' *Journal of African Languages* 11, 3: 21-47.

Chisukwa: a related dialect

Kershner, Tiffany L. 2001. "Imperfectivity in Chisukwa." In R. Botne and R. Vondrasek (eds.), *Explorations in African Linguistics: From Lamnso' to Sesotho* (Working Papers in Linguistics 3), IULC: Bloomington, IN. Pp. 37-52.

Kershner, Tiffany L. 2002. The verb in Chisukwa: Aspect, tense, and time. Ph.d. dissertation, Indiana University.

PART 1

PHONOLOGY

❖ Vowels

• The vowel system

Chindali exhibits five distinct vowel qualities, each with short and long counterparts. Long vowels are represented orthographically as a sequence of two identical vowels. Examples of each, contrasting each vowel quality in short and long form both in verb roots and nouns, are listed below.

Short i, e, a, o, u		Long ii, ee, aa, oo, uu	
Verb stems			
-tima	'become wet'	*-tiima*	'graze cattle'
-kema	'crack'	*-keema*	'grunt'
-kaba	'earn'	*-kaaba*	'be late'
-kola	'touch; hold'	*-koola*	'cough'
-futa	'shape dough into a ball'	*-fuuta*	'breathe'
Nouns			
ichi.lílo	'mourning'	*ichí.liílo*	'luggage'
íi.sele	'creeping plant'	*ú.seéle*	'hammerkop'
iin.dáfu	'morning breath'	*ín.daáfu*	'locust'
umú.kolo	'woman'	*umú.koólo*	'small hoe'
íchi.kuku	'big chicken'	*ichi.kúuku*	'dove'

• Vowel length

Vowel length is distinctive, as the preceding set of examples illustrate. Length also appears to be distinctive, at least for some speakers, preceding NC clusters or following glides, environments typically inducing vowel lengthening in most Bantu languages. For example, one finds:

ngímba 'Question marker'	*ngíimba* 'yet'
ichí.mwemwe 'smile'	*uku.mwemwéétela* 'smile'

Vowels often remain short, or are shortened, in both pre-NC and post-glide environments when there is a following long vowel.

u.lembaléemba	'spider's nest'
ichi.ndundúúnga	'large, deep basket'
u.kambóoni	'marriage representative'
nganíngaáni	'especially'

7

Augment vowels of certain noun prefixes are lengthened when there are fewer than two moras in the noun stem. Thus, class 1a *u-*, class 5a *i-*, and classes 9 and 10 *in-* undergo such lengthening, as in the examples below.

1a	*úú.bubi*	'spider'	*u.bóoto*	'mudfish'
	u.chímye	'quiet person'	*ú.chipili*	'puff-adder'
5a	*ií.bwe*	'rock'	*i.bíingu*	'cloud'
	ií.pele	'type of beer'	*í.pelele*	'dry maize stalk'
9/10	*iíngwi*	'firewood'	*in.gwíina*	'crocodile'
	iin.dáfu	'morning breath'	*ín.daáfu*	'locust'
	ii.síla	'path'	*í.siíla*	'other side'

• Vowel coalescence and elision

Vowels frequently come into contact at morpheme boundaries, both in nouns and verbs. In such cases, the first of the two vowels typically under-goes a change. Within a word, the vowels /i/ and /u/ become glides, although in some cases before back round vowels /u/ may be deleted. The vowel /a/ is typically deleted if it occurs in prefixal elements, but coalesces with the vowel if it occurs in the root.

i + i	> yi	*ify.íisu* {ifi-}	'countries'	u + i	> wi	*úlw.iiba* {úlu-}	'grass'
i + e	> ye	*ímy.eéndo* {ími-}	'thighs'	u + e	> we	*ukw.éega* {uku-}	'get'
i + a	> ya	*ukú.lya* {-li-}	'to eat'	u + a	> wa	*kw.áábo* {ku-}	'their home'
i + o	> yo	*íly.ooto* {íli-}	'ashes'	u + o	> wo	*úmw.ooga* {úmu-}	'coward'
i + u	> yu	*ímy.uugi* {ími-}	'vapors'		> o	*uk.óoga* {uku-}	'wash'
				u + u	> wu	*úmw.uugi* {úmu-}	'vapor'
					> u	*uk.úuma* {uku-}	'be dry'

8

With the prefixes *chi-* and *shi-*, the vowel /i/ is deleted in all cases, e.g., *ich.íisu* 'country'. With the prefix *bu-*, the vowel /u/ is realized as a velar fricative, hence, [υ^γi], e.g., *úbw.iifi* [úu$^\gamma$iːfi] 'theft'. Before /o/ and /u/, both *bu-* and *mu-* are variable in their realizations, with the vowel sometimes deleted, sometimes elided.

The vowel /a/ is deleted from prefixes when it occurs before any vowel, e.g., *ám.eele* 'bow', or *éega* 'he has married' [a-aa-eeg-a 3S-ANT-marry]. If the vowel is part of a root, it coalesces with the [i] of the APPLICATIVE, e.g., *-peela* [-pa- 'give' + -il- APP], but is deleted before the [i] of the completive aspect *-ile*, e.g., *-piile*.

In cases of vowel contact across word boundaries, the final vowel of the first word is typically deleted in normal, rapid speech.

• Vowel harmony (assimilation)

There are two patterns of vowel assimilation, both occurring in verb suffixes. One involves an [i]/[e] alternation, the other an [u]/[o] alternation.

• [i] / [e] alternation

The vowel in certain verb suffixes alternates in quality depending on the quality of the vowel preceding it. The front vowel /i/ alternates with /e/, /e/ occurring following the mid-vowels /e/ and /o/.

-ik- ~ -ek-

IMPOSITIVE:

-fub-ik-a	'soak in water'	*-gon-ek-a*	'lay s.o. down'
-baamb-ik-a	'put in a line'		

MEDIO-PASSIVE:

-piind-ik-a	'be bent'	*-bon-ek-a*	'be visible'
-mal-ik-a	'be used up'		

-il- ~ -el-

APPLICATIVE:

-fik-il-a	'settle'	*-kes-el-a*	'bark at'
-suk-il-a	'wash for'	*-gon-el-a*	'lie on'
-taang-il-a	'precede'		

-ilil- ~ -elel-

PERSISTIVE:

-kiind-ilil-a	'rush'	*-keet-elel-a*	'watch'
-buuk-ilil-a	'go beyond'		

9

-ish- ~ -esh-

    EFFERENTIAL:

    -lil-ish-a   'make cry'

    -gul-ish-a   'sell'   *-kop-esh-a*   'lend'

    -many'-ish-a   'teach, inform'

    INTENSIVE:

    -paal-ish-a   'thank s.o.'   *-keet-esh-a*   'inspect closely'

- [u] / [o] alternation

The second pattern of assimilation occurs with the vowel /u/, which alternates with /o/. In this case, /o/ occurs only when the preceding vowel is also /o/.

-up- ~ -op-

    STATIVE:

    -eel-up-a   'be white'

    -buul-up-a   'be faded'   *-soong-op-a*   'be sharp'

-uk- ~ -ok-

    SEPARATIVE (MDEIO-PASSIVE):

    -iin-uk-a   'be upright'

    -pul-uk-a   'drop off'   *-ny'oong-ok-a*   'break off'

    -sat-uk-a   'tear'

-ul- ~ -ol-

    SEPARATIVE (ACTIVE):

    -iin-ul-a   'turn upright'

    -pul-ul-a   'pick off'   *-ny'oong-ol-a*   'break off'

    -sat-ul-a   'tear'

❖ **Consonants**

- **Consonant inventory**

Chindali has an inventory of seventeen phonemes. Of these, /z/ is extremely rare. [ʒ], orthographically *j*, is found in the Tanzanian variety of Chindali; the equivalent in Malawi is [j], orthographically *y*.

	Bilabial	Labio-dental	Alveolar	(Alveo-)Palatal	Velar	Glottal
Stops						
−vox			t		k	
Affricates						
−vox				tʃ		
Fricatives						
−vox	ʋ	f	s	ʃ	ɣ	h
+vox			z	[ʒ]		
Nasal	m		n	ɲ	ŋ	
Approximant	w		l	y		

an optional allophonic variant of /l/ is [ɹ]: l → ɹ / {i, e}__

(ɰ) = variant of /ɣ/

The palatal nasal /ɲ/, written *ny'*, is distinct from the very similar pala-talized nasal [nʸ], written *ny*. In slow, careful speech, the palatalized nasal sounds much like [ni]; however, there is no mora associated with it.

• **Nasal + consonant assimilation**

There are four nasal+consonant combinations that occur: mb, nd, ɲj, ŋg. In each case, the nasal is homorganic with the stop. These prenasalized stops occur inherently as part of the root or stem, or they may be derived as nasal and consonant come into contact at morpheme boundaries. Derivational pat-terns, with examples, are provided in the chart below.

mb	<	N + ʋ	*iiny'áma íim.bisi*	'uncooked meat'
			< -bisi	'uncooked'
nd	<	N + t	*in.déefu*	'mats'
			< ulu.téefu	'mat'
		N + l	*in.dagílo*	'rules'
			< ulu.lagílo	'rule'
nj [nʒ]	<	N + y	*in.jébo*	'gossip'
			< ulu.yébo	
ŋg	<	N + k	*iín.gáma*	'milk'
			< ulú.kǎma	'milk'
		N + ɣ	*imbáale ín.galamu*	'flat plate'
			< -galamu	'flat'

11

The nasal becomes deleted when it precedes a spirant or another nasal, as illustrated in the examples below from classes 11/10 /ulu-, in-/ and 9/10 /in-, in-/.

ulu.fúkwe	*ii.fúkwe*	'belly/s'
ulu.séba	*ii.séba*	'sacred hut/s'
ulú.shííla	*í.shííla*	'fallow land/s'
i.máanga	*i.máanga*	'mango/es'
ulú.nuunda	*í.nuunda*	'fishing spear/s'
ii.ng'óma	*ii.ng'óma*	'drum/s'

• **Imbrication**

The completive aspect suffix *-ite* is typically affixed to the end of the verbal stem. However, in certain instances it is phonologically incorporated, or imbricated, into the stem itself. This occurs regularly when the stem-final consonant is [l]. There is also at least one irregular instance occurring with a stem-final nasal.

In imbrication, the vowel [i] of *-ite* appears before the final consonant of the verb stem, while the consonant is not realized at all, hence, ...CV_{stem} - i - l - e. If the stem vowel, V_{stem}, is a non-round vowel /i, e, a/, the V_{stem} is deleted and the /i/ lengthened. If the V_{stem} is a round vowel, it becomes [w] and the /i/ again lengthens. In the irregular case of the verb *-many'a*, the [a] and [i] coalesce to form a long [eː].

-biyila	>	*-biyiile*	*-many'a*	>	*-meeny'e*
-bonela	>	*-boniile*	*-bona*	>	*-bweeni*
-aangala	>	*-aangiile*			
-fyoogola	>	*-fyoogwiile*			
-aabula	>	*-aabwiile*			

A similar phenomenon is found with stem final *-il-* plus persistive *-ilil-*.

-il- + -ilil- > -iilil-

-pitila	>	*-pitiilila*	'oversleep'
-gonela	>	*-goneelela*	'sleep too long'

❖ **Syllable structure**

The canonical syllable structure in the language can be considered to be CV. However, there are ten syllable types, distinguished by structure and vowel length.

Type	Short V			Long V	
V	*ú.ka.lu.lu*	'hare'		*ií.ge*	'egg'
CV	*ii.kó.kwe*	'tree'		*u.bíí.sa*	'rooster'
C^GV	*chi.mye*	'quietly'		*ú.mwií.fwa*	'thorn'
^NCV	*íi.mbe.po*	'wind'		*í.mbee.mbe*	'horn'
^NC^GV	*ií.ngwi*	'firewood'		*í.ngwaa.pa*	'armpit'
Ṇ	*n.di*	'I say'			

❖ Tonal phenomena

Chindali is a (restricted) tone language, meaning that certain vowel positions may exhibit variation in pitch and that this variation may be distinctive, lexically or grammatically. There are four realizations of pitch—High, Low, Rise, Fall, and Downstepped High—which can be analyzed in terms of the placement of an underlying high tone on a particular mora in the word. Downstepped highs on long vowels often arise from a rising tone. Under this view, long vowels consist of two moras, either or both of which may be assigned a high tone.

Register tones:

High (V́)	*ulu.báfu*	'rib'
Low (unmarked)	*kwaambula*	'without'

Contour tones:

Rise (VV́) [occurs only on long vowels]

	initial	*ií.swi*	'fish'
	following a High	*pamúpeéne*	'together'

Fall (V́V) [only occurs on long vowels] *ichi.fúukwa* 'reason'

Downstepped tones:

High ('CV́) or ('CV́V́)

	aka.bóꜜléla	'beesting'
	pamúꜜpééne	'together'
	ú.ꜜbééngu	'liver'

• Nouns

Nouns have, at most, two high tones, typically just one. Although tones may be a minimal feature distinguishing lexical items, as in the pairs listed below, there appear to be relatively few such pairs in the language.

ama.séengo	'poles for building'	*im.bóombo*	'work'
amá.seéngo	'horns for medicine'	*ím.boómbo*	'navel'
ubw.óoga	'mushroom'	*in.góóndo*	'back of head'
úbw.ooga	'fear'	*ín.goondo*	'base of tree'
ichi.páanga	'church'	*ulu.fúundo*	'punishment'
ichí.paanga	'cavern'	*ulú.fuundo*	'knot'

More commonly, nouns will differ as well in at least one phone, either in the nominal root or in the nominal prefix.

iin.góle	'vein'	*iim.bága*	'dew'
íin.golo	'louse'	*íchi.baga*	'byre'

Tone patterns [mora-based]:

Penultimate	Ante-penult	Pre-ante-penult	Ante- & penult	Pre-ante- & penult
VCV́.C(G)V	—	—	—	—
VV́N.C(G)V	—	—	—	—
VV́.C(G)V	—	—	—	—
VCV.CV́CV	VCV́.CVCV	V́CV.CVCV	VCV́.CV́CV	??
VVN.CV́CV	V́V́N.CVCV	V́VN.CVCV	V́V́N.CV́CV	V́VN.CV́CV
VV.CV́CV	V́V́.CVCV	V́V.CVCV	V́V́.CV́CV	??
VCV.CV́V́CV	VCV.CV́VCV	VCV́.CVVCV	VCV́.CVV́CV	??
VN.CV́V́CV	VN.CV́VCV	V́N.CVVCV	V́N.CVV́CV	—
V.CV́V́CV	V.CV́VCV	V́.CVVCV	V́.CVV́CV	—

Penultimate	Ante-penult	Pre-ante- & penult
VCV.CVCV́CV	VCV.CV́CVCV	VCV́.CVCVCV
VN.CVCV́CV	VN.CV́CVCV	V́N.CVCVCV
V.CVCV́CV	??	V́.CVCVCV

14

	Ante- & penult	Pre-ante- & penult
	VCV.CV́CV́CV	VCV́.CVCV́CV
	??	??
	V.CV́CV́CV	??

Penultimate	Ante-penult	Stem-initial	Pre-stem
VCV.CVCVCV́C V	VCV.CVCV́CVC V	??	VCV́.CVCVCVCV
			V́CV.CVCVCVCV
VN.CVCVCV́CV	??	??	V́N.CVCVCVCV
V.CVCVCV́CV	??	V.CV́CVCVCV	V́.CVCVCVCV

• Verbs

Infinitival forms of verbs, i.e., class 15 forms with prefix *uku-*, have a high tone on the ante-penultimate mora, with the exception of monosyllabic stems, in which the high tone appears on *-ku-* in the prefix.

ukú.kwa	'pay dowry'		
ukú.kola	'touch'	*uku.kóola*	'shout'
uku.kóleka	'make s.o. hold'	*uku.kóólela*	'shout loudly'
uku.kolákola	'feel'	*uku.koláana*	'resemble'

An apparent exception to this pattern is found with the causative (-*y*-) and passive (-*w*-) suffixes. In these cases, the tone appears on the vowel immediately preceding the suffix. However, assuming the underlying form of the suffix contributes a mora, the tone on the verb would still be, underlyingly, on the ante-penultimate mora, as in the cases above.

uku.kúsha	'bring up a child'	[< *ukú.kula* 'grow up']
uku.kopésha	'lend'	[< *ukú.kopa* 'borrow']
[compare non-causative *uku.kópesha* 'beckon']		
uku.kópwa	'be owed'	[< *ukú.kopa* 'borrow']

The high tone does not appear if the verb is followed by an object.

ukuseenga iny'úumba	'to build a house'
ukubega íchipapa	'to cut the skin'
ukubuuka kuChúuba	'to go to Chuba'
ukubuuka kuchípataala	'to go to the hospital'

15

High tone may also play a grammatical role. The addition of a high tone may function to distinguish between attributive and predicative uses of possessives. The absence of the augment in conjuction with a shift in the position of the high tone functions either to change adjectives from an attributive to a predicative relation, or to change a simple noun to a presentative predicate.

íimbushi yáangu	'my sheep'	[Attributive]
íimbushi yáángu	'the sheep is mine/it's my sheep'	[Predicative]
amálíma ámabisi	'uncooked beans'	[Attributive]
amálíma mábisi	'the beans are uncooked'	[Predicative]
úmwaana úmukulu	'a fat child'	[Attributive]
úmwaana múkulu	'the child is fat'	[Predicative]
úmwaana	'child'	
mwáana	's/he's a child'	[Presentative]

The placement of a high tone may also be a function of the tense or tenor in which it occurs. Although most tenses assign a high tone to the ante-penultimate mora, as found in the simple verb infinitive, some assign a high to other positions.

ga-pííle	'it's [water] hot' [now]
g-aa-píile	'it [water] was hot' [this morning]

16

PART 2

NOUN MORPHOLOGY

❖ The noun class system

Chindali has a system comprising 18 noun classes. These classes consist of three types of nouns: nouns proper, verbal nouns, and locative nouns. The first type comprises 14 noun classes, some of which include sub-classes; the second includes only one class, traditionally numbered 15 by Bantuists; the third consists of three locative classes, traditionally numbered 16-18. Each is described in turn below.

With few exceptions, all nouns have a nominal class prefix (NPfx), e.g., *u.lu.kama* 'milk'. The NPfx may be preceded by an augment vowel identical to the prefix vowel, if there is one. A few nouns do not have a prefix, consisting only of a root, as in *zeenje* 'outhouse, latrine'. Prefixes do not have inherent tones; rather, the tone varies according to the word.

The form of the class prefix varies according to the phonological features of the initial segment of the noun stem.

• Nouns proper

There are three general types of prefixes on nouns:

V-	i-, u-
VCV-	a.ba-, a.ka-, a.ma-, i.chi-, i.fi-, i.li-, i.mi-, u.bu-, u.lu-, u.mu-, u.tu-
iN-	i.n-, i.m-

With the exception of the V- prefixes, each consists of a potential vocalic augment plus the class prefix proper, shown in Table 2.1.

• Verbal nouns (infinitives)

Verbal nouns exhibit characteristics of both nouns and verbs. Like nouns, they require a class prefix, *uku-*, of the same kind as ordinary nouns. Like other nouns, verbal nouns effect agreement with modifying elements such as adjectives, the linking connective *-aa*, and verbs. Unlike other nouns, however, the tone of verbal nouns is grammatically determined: a high tone appears on the ante-penultimate mora (or immediately preceding a causative or passive suffix, if there is one). See Table 2.2.

Verbal nouns also exhibit verbal characteristics and, consequently, function much like infinitives or gerunds. They may mark objects, take verbal suffixes, and have no high tone if there is a following object.

*uku-**mu**-liisha íígesha*	'to feed him/her porridge'
uku-lekéésha	'to cease temporarily' [< ukú-leka 'cease']

19

Table 2.1 Noun class prefixes[1]

CLASS	CL PFX		
1	*u.mu-, u.muu-, u.mw-*	*úmukolo*	'woman'
1a	*u-, uu-, w-*	*umbúgulu*	'owl'
2	*a.ba-, a.baa-, a.b-*	*abáliisha*	'men'
2a	*a.boo-*	*abóópafwa*	'lungs'
3	*u.mu-, u.mw-*	*umútu*	'head'
4	*i.mi-, i.my-*	*imipáka*	'borders'
5	*i-, ii-*	*ípelele*	'maize stalk'
5a	*i.li-, i.ly-*	*ilíshu*	'voice'
6	*a.ma-, amaa-, a.m-*	*ámafupa*	'bones'
7	*i.chi-, i.chii-, i.ch-*	*ichilóonda*	'wound'
8	*i.fi-, i.fy-*	*ifíloómbe*	'maize'
9	*i.ny'-, i.n-, i.m-, i.ŋ-, i-*	*íny'oobe*	'finger'
10	*i.ny'-, i.n-, i.m-, i.ŋ-, i-*	*indagílo*	'rules'
11	*u.lu-, u.lw-*	*ulufúkwe*	'belly'
12	*a.ka-, a.kaa-, a.k-*	*ákakono*	'arm'
13	*u.tu-, u.tw-*	*utúlo*	'sleep'
14	*u.bu-, u.buu-, u.bw-*	*ubumany'íli*	'education'

Table 2.2 Verbal noun prefixes

CLASS	CL PFX		
15	*u.ku-, u.kw-, uk-*	*ukú-gula*	'to buy; buying'
		uku-gulísha	'to sell; selling'

Table 2.3 Locative prefixes

CLASS	CL PFX		
16	*pa-, paa-, p-*	*pamupáando*	'at/on the chair'
17	*ku-, kuu-, kw-*	*kuKaróonga*	'to Karonga'
18	*mu-, muu-, mw-*	*muchisány'a*	'in the dry season'

---

[1] Kishindo (1998) includes a Class 21 *ili-* that is used to derive augmentattive or pejorative nouns. I did not come across this class in my own research.

• **Locative nouns**

Locative prefixes express a general spatial relationship between two objects. Although they are translated with English prepositions, they do not correlate exactly with the meaning of the English word. Class 16 *pa-* expresses a relation of contact, the exact nature determined from the verb and context, e.g., *-eegamila pamupáando* 'lean against the chair'. Class 17 *ku-* typically expresses movement toward the object, e.g., *-mweegamisha kulúbuumba* 'make him lean against the wall'. Finally, Class 18 *mu-* expresses interiority, e.g., *-ya mututeengéle* 'go into the woods'. See Table 2.3.

The locative prefixes occur in the same position as the augment, hence, the noun cannot have both an augment and a locative prefix. Long vowel forms occur with stems that have two or fewer moras: *paanyúma* 'at/in back' (cf. *pándaashi* 'in front').

❖ **Nominal genders**

Nouns typically occur in singular/plural pairings, called genders, of which there are 10 primary ones in Chindali. Sub-classes, which require the same agreement patterns, are subsumed under the main gender pairing, hence, 1a-2a under 1-2. Although most nouns occur as singular/plural pairings of two noun classes, as listed in Table 2.4, there are some nouns that occur only in one noun class. These single-class genders are listed in Table 2.5.

Many genders include at least one coherent semantic concept underlying a set of nouns found in that gender. The concept may be inclusive, e.g, all nouns in Gender I are human, or represent a small but discernible portion of items, e.g., body parts in Gender IV.

❖ **The augment**

The augment is a prefixed vowel that precedes the noun-class prefix, e.g., the initial [a] of *a.ma-* or the initial [i] of *i.fi-*. This vowel is identical to that found in the class prefix. It is not obligatory, and does not appear in certain environments:

- when a locative prefix is attached to the noun,
- when the noun follows the connective linker *-aa,*
- when the noun follows any form of the verb 'be', i.e., *-ba* or *-li,*
- when the noun follows the conjunction *ngáti* 'like',
- when the noun follows the complementizer *ukúti* 'that',
- when the noun follows the defective verb *-ti* 'say'.

21

Table 2.4 Noun genders: Paired singular/plural classes

Gender	Classes	Prefixes Singular	Prefixes Plural	Semantic nexus
I	1/2	*u.mu-*	*a.ba-*	humans
Ia	1a/2a	*u-*	*a.boo-*	kin older than ego; special humans; animals
II	3/4	*u.mu-*	*i.mi-*	linear or planar items; natural phenomena
III	5/6	*i-*	*a.ma-*	items in natural sets or groups
IIIa	5a/6	*i.li-*	*a.ma-*	
IV	7/8	*i.chi-*	*i.fi-*	tools, body parts; segments of whole; augmentative
V	9/6	*i.N-*	*a.ma-*	
VI	9/10	*i.N-*	*i.N-*	foods; animals
VII	11/6	*u.lu-*	*a.ma-*	
VIII	11/10	*u.lu-*	*i.N-*	
IX	12/13	*a.ka-*	*u.tu-*	diminutive
X	14/6	*u.bu-*	*a.ma-*	

Table 2.5 Noun genders: Non-paired noun classes

Gender	Class	Prefix	Semantic nexus
Iax	1a	*u-*	drinks; diseases
IIx	2	*a.ba-*	humans
IIIx	3	*u.mu-*	linear or planar items
IVx	4	*i.mi-*	pejorative
Vx	5	*i-*	
Vax	5a	*i.li-*	
VI	6	*a.ma-*	liquids; pasty, powdery, granular substances
VII	7	*i.chi-*	languages; emotions
VIII	8	*i.fi-*	
IX	9	*i.N-*	diseases
X	10	*i.N-*	
XI	11	*u.lu-*	
XII	12	*a.ka-*	manner of doing
XIII	13	*u.tu-*	small quantity; diminutive
XIV	14	*u.bu-*	abstract concepts

❖ Nominal derivation

Nouns can be derived from verbs by the addition of an appropriate class prefix and, typically, a specific stem-final vowel.

• Agentives

Agentive nouns denote the doer of an action. They are derived from verbs by affixing to the verb stem a gender I prefix, *umu-/aba-*, in conjunction with the suffix *-i* or *-aayi*. There is a high tone typically on the penultimate syllable, realized as falling if the vowel is long.

umu.kéet.i	'witness'	<	*-keeta*	'look'
umu.ny'amúl.i	'porter'	<	*-ny'amula*	'carry'
umu.páap.i	'parent'	<	*-paapa*	'produce a child'
umu.yúg.i	'spokesperson'	<	*-yuga*	'speak'
umu.mog.áayi	'dancer'	<	*-moga*	'dance'
umu.kwees.áayi	'heavy smoker'	<	*-kweesa*	'smoke'

In two cases, the same verb stem has different meanings with the different suffixes.

umw.íimb.i	'singer'	<	*-iimba*	'sing; perform'
umw.iimb.áayi	'performer'			
umu.mát.i	'potter'	<	*-mata*	'mould clay'
umu.mat.áayi	'one who works with clay'			

• Attributives

Attributive nouns denote a person who has the characteristic attribute conveyed by the verb it is derived from. The derived noun has a Gender I prefix, *umu-/aba-*, in conjunction with a suffixed *-e*. There is a high tone, invariably on the prefix.

úmu.bin.e	'sick person'	<	*-bina*	'become sick'
úmu.gom.e	'old person'	<	*-goma*	'become old'
umú.lemal.e	'lame person'	<	*-lemala*	'become lame'
umú.sekel.e	'happy person'	<	*-sekela*	'be happy'
umú.fw.e	'dead person'	<	*-fwa*	'die'
umú.fwiilw.e	'kin of deceased'	<	*-fwiila*	'die APPL'

• Experiencers

Experiencer nouns refer to humans who have been subjected to some action or event. The noun has a Gender I prefix, *umu-/aba-*, with final *-a*, unless the stem-final consonant is [b], in which case it is *-u* (and the [ʋ] becomes [f]. A high tone typically appears on the ante-penultimate mora.

umu.pĩin.a	'poor person'	<	*-piina*	'lack'
umu.kúúngiw.a	'arrested person'·	<	*-kuungiwa*	'be arrested'
umu.kíf.u	'one who endures pain'	<	*-kiba*	'endure pain'

• Manner of behaving

Manner nouns refer to the way in which the named behavior is carried out. The derived noun takes Gender IX prefixes, *aka-/utu-*, with a final *-e* or *-o*. It also is based on the applied form of the stem. A high tone appears on the first or second mora of the prefix with *-e* final nouns, on the penultimate mora with *-o* final nouns.

aká.mogel.e	'manner of dancing'	<	*-moga*	'dance'
aká.fwaalil.e	'manner of dressing'	<	*-fwaala*	'dress'
ák.eengel.e	'manner of brewing'	<	*-eenga*	'brew'
ák.iikalil.e	'manner of living'	<	*-iikala*	'exist'
ak.iinong'onél.o	'manner of thinking'	<	*-iinong'ona*	'think'
aka.limíl.o	'manner of cultivating'	<	*-lima*	'cultivate'

• Nominalized actions

Nouns denoting the concrete entity performed by the action of the verb are derived from the verb by affixing either the Gender VI prefixes *ulu-/iN-* or the Gender V prefixes *iN-/iN-* and suffixing *-o* to the stem. There appears to be no regularity to the placement of a high tone.

• Gender VI derivations

úlw.iimb.o	'song'	<	*-iimba*	'sing'
ulu.komáan.o	'meeting'	<	*-komaana*	'meet'
ulu.lagíl.o	'rule'	<	*-lagila*	'rule'

• Gender V derivations

iny'.iipúut.o	'prayer'	<	*-iipuuta*	'pray'
ín.gulum.o	'thunder'	<	*-guluma*	'thunder'
im.bóomb.o	'work'	<	*-boomba*	'do; work'

24

• Liquids

Nouns referring to liquids are derived by affixing the class 6 prefix *ama-* and suffixing a final *-i* to the appropriate verb stem. A high tone appears on the penultimate syllable.

ama.tapísh.i	'vomitus'	<	*-tapika*	'vomit'
ama.túush.i	'urine'	<	*-tuunda*	'urinate'

• Means

Nouns denoting the means used to carry out the action indicated by the verb are derived in several ways. All take a final *-o*, while the gender of the prefixes may differ. First, they may affix the Gender III prefixes, *i-/ama-*, second, the Gender IV prefixes, *ichi-/ifi-*; third, the Gender V prefixes, *iN-/iN-*; fourth, the Gender IX prefixes, *aka-/utu-*. A high tone typically appears on the penultimate mora.

• Gender III derivation

i.poondél.o	'foundry'	<	*-poonda*	'forge'

• Gender IV derivations

ichi.lwíil.o	'weapon'	<	*-lwiila*	'fight by use of'
ichi.many'ísh.o	'lesson'	<	*-many'isha*	'teach'
ichi.sekesél.o	'sieve'	<	*-sekesa*	'sift'
ich.áánik.o	'place for drying'	<	*-aanika*	'set out to dry'
ich.aambúk.o	'place to ford'	<	*-aambuka*	'cross a river'

• Gender V derivations

iim.bósh.o	'medicine'	<	*-posha*	'heal'
i.soongolél.o	'stick for digging'	<	*-soongola*	'sharpen'
i.suuyíl.o	'strainer'	<	*-suuya*	'strain'

• Gender IX derivations

aka.pekés.o	'stick rubbed to make fire'	<	*-pekesa*	'rub sticks'
aka.shéél.o	'grindstone wheel'	<	*-sha*	'grind'

• Materials

Nouns denoting the material used to perform an action are derived affixing either Gender III prefixes *i(ly)-/ama-* or Gender V prefixes *iN-/iN-* with suffix *-o* attached to the stem.

25

• Gender III derivations

i.léemb.o	'letter of the alphabet'	<	*-leemba*	'write'
íly.oong.o	'breast milk'	<	*-oonga*	'suck breast'

• Gender V derivations

i.fwáal.o	'clothes'	<	*-fwaala*	'dress'
i.séeng.o	'pole for building'	<	*-seenga*	'build'

• Abstract concepts

Abstract nouns are derived from verbs by adding the class 14 prefix *ubu-* and either final *-e* or *-i*. With *-e* final nouns, a high tone always appears on the prefix, with final *-i* on the penultimate syllable.

ubú.fw.e	'death'	<	*-fwa*	'die'
úbu.bin.e	'illness'	<	*-bina*	'become ill'
ubú.pulikan.e	'understanding'	<	*-pulikana*	'agree'
úbw.iigan.e	'pleasure'	<	*-iigana*	'like'
ubu.mány'.i	'knowledge'	<	*-many'a*	'know'
ubu.chulúsh.i	'business'	<	*-chulusha*	'sell'
ubw.íim.i	'selfishness'	<	*-iima*	'refuse to give'

❖ **Construct nouns**

Nouns can be constructed from other nouns by attaching a noun class prefix— typically from class 1 or class 7 (or their correlative plurals)—to the connective linker *-aa*, which is cliticized to the augmentless form of the noun, hence, V́C-aa=NPfx.STEM. Depending on the class prefix attached, the sense becomes 'one of N' or 'thing of N'.

• NPfx plus linker plus common noun

úw.aa=chi.páanga	'church-goer'	<	*ichi.páanga*	'church'
úw.aa=lú.ko	'relative'	<	*ulú.ko*	'clan'
ích.aa=bú.tuuli	'aid'	<	*ubú.tuuli*	'help'

• NPfx plus linker plus locative noun

ích.aa=pá.k.aaya	'household item'	<	*pá.k.aaya*	'at home'
ák.aa=pa.m.boómbo	'umbilical cord'	<	*pa.m.boómbo*	'at the navel'
úw.aa=pa.mu.páando	'chairman'	<	*pa.mu.páando*	'on the chair'
útw.aa=mu.chí.póso	'small things from the bush'	<	*mu.chí.póso*	'in the bush'

• NPfx plus linker plus verbal noun

ích.aa=kú.ly.a	'food'	<	*-lya*	'eat'
ích.aa=kú.ng'w.a	'drink'	<	*-ng'wa*	'drink'
ích.aa=ku.pííyil.a	'utensil for cooking'	<	*-piiyila*	'cook with'

❖ **Compound nouns**

Compound nouns are formed in one of two ways: noun plus noun or verb plus noun. Most compounds, of which only about two dozen have been identified, refer to humans. Noun plus noun compounds are rare; most are built on the noun *úmw.eéne* 'owner'. Noun plus verb compounds affix the appropriate noun class prefix to the verb stem. In some cases, the noun in the compound is no longer extant in the language.

• Noun + noun

umu.fwámaaso 'blind person'	<	*umú,fwe* 'dead' + *ámaa.so* 'eyes'
umw.enechíisu 'owner of land'	<	*úmw.eéne* 'owner' + *ich.íisu* 'land'
umw.enékaaya 'head of family'	<	*úmw.eéne* 'owner' + *ák.aaya* 'home'
umw.enémwaana 'guardian of a child'	<	*úmw.eéne* 'owner' + *úmw.aana* 'child'

• Verb + noun

umu.paalíny'iimbo 'song leader'	<	*-paala* 'lead' + *íiny'iimbo* 'song'
umu.pelilyóoyo 'annoying person'	<	*-pela* 'create' + *ily.óoyo* 'temper'

umu.tulánoongwa   <   *-tula* 'be guilty' + *í.noongwa* 'fault'
'sinner'

umu.pelachísa   <   *-pela* 'create' + *ichí.sa* 'compassion'
'pitiful person'

u.mukoláánguku   <   *-kola 'catch'* + *íín.guku* 'chicken'
'sp. of wild cat'

❖ **Reduplicated nouns**

Reduplication does not appear to be a productive process for creating nouns. There is, however, a relatively small but significant set of nouns in the language exhibiting some form of reduplication. The base for reduplication, with one exception, is the stem, which may be partially or fully reduplicated. In the one exceptional case, the word is the basis for reduplication.

• Reduplication of the stem in doubly prefixed nouns

Two nouns exhibit apparent partial reduplication of the stem. However, in both cases, the initial part of the stem that is not reduplicated represents an earlier noun prefix that is now part of the stem.

| *u.ka.shúushu* | 'bat' | *ichíí.n.gwiíkwi* | 'butterfly' |

• Full reduplication of the stem

Full reduplication occurs with monosyllabic or disyllabic stems. Each type can be further differentiated according to the length of the penultimate vowel.

Monosyllabic stems

ichí.mwemwe	'smile'	*íchi.papa*	'animal hide'
ubu.líli	'fine mat'	*áma.susu*	'chicken dung'
u.byéébye	'bird of prey'	*ulu.séese*	'udder'
ulu.ny'áany'a	'tomato'	*ichi.píipi*	'fritter'
ulu.ny'éeny'e	'bumblebee'		
u.ng'áang'a	'sp. of bird'	*ubú.poopo*	'carelessness'

28

Disyllabic stems

umu.fuláfúla	sp. of tree	*í.fwalafwala*	'liver'
umu.subásúba	sp. of tree	*ím.bulubulu*	'tadpole'
		ichí.bubabuba	'bat'
		aká.fulufulu	'whirlwind'
umu.chefuchéfu	'clever person'	*umú.gulugulu*	'untrustworthy person'
i.lambílaámbi	'tree bark'	*u.lembaléemba*	'spider's nest'
im.buungápuúnga	'corn tassel'	*im.bilipíili*	'hot pepper'
umu.lombéloómbe	'maize leaf'	*u.ny'elany'éela*	type of dance
umu.chiinjáchiínja	'murderer'	*u.polepóole*	type of dance
		umu.piingopíingo	'rainbow'
aka.sangasáánga	'hay'	*ubw.oolóolo*	'politeness'

• Full reduplication of the word

In one case, the full word, minus the augment, is the base for reduplication. This process adds the sense of "real" to the meaning of the noun.

abaa.ndúbáándu	'real people'	< *abáa.ndu*	'people'

• Partial reduplication of the stem

In partial reduplication, only the first CV of the stem is reduplicated.

ichi.papáátula	'bark for firewood'	*ichi.pépeéla*	'place to wash'
umu.seséénga	'sand'	*umú.totófulu*	'foam'
amaa.shíshííla	'soot'		

❖ **Reduplicative compounding**

Two instances of reduplicative compounding have been noted. These involve reduplication of a locative noun, contributing the sense of 'various'.

mufibága mufibága	'in various sections'	cf. *ifibága* 'sections'
mumabúyo mumabúyo	'in various places'	cf. *amabúyo* 'places'

soóna kwoope ukúmoga, tuumoga mumabúyo mumabúyo
'furthermore, when dancing, we dance in various places'

29

❖ Evaluative nouns

Evaluative nouns include augmentatives, pejoratives, diminutives and approbatives, that is, variations on the basic noun that indicate the speaker's judgment in terms of size or quality. The new noun is derived by adding an appropriate prefix. These are productive processes.

* Augmentatives

Augmentatives are derived by replacing the original gender prefixes with the Gender IV prefixes *ichi-/ifi-*. In a few cases, the original noun no longer exists.

íchi.kuku	'large chicken'	<	*íin.guku*	'chicken'
ichi.bwíina	'pit'	<	*ubw.íina*	'hole'
ichíí.fuúni	'shadow from a large object'	⇔	*akáá.fuúni*	'shade from a small object'

* Pejoratives

Pejoratives are derived by replacing the original gender prefixes with the Gender II prefixes *umu-/imi-*. BIG reflects a sense of 'oversized'.

umu.kúúmbe	'big/ugly pot'	<	*in.gúúmbe*	'clay pot'
umu.kwáama	'big/ugly sack'	<	*ichi.kwáama*	'sack'
umu.lombéloómbe	'big/ugly maize plant'	<	*ichí.loómbe*	'maize plant'
imíi.ndu	'mess'	<	*ichíí.ndu*	'thing'

* Diminutives and approbatives

Diminutives and approbatives are derived in the same way as the above, except that they replace the original gender prefixes with the Gender IX prefixes *aka-/utu-*.

aka.fúúngúla	'bunch of bananas'	<	*umu.fúúngúla*	'stalk'
aká.paále	'small calabash'	<	*ichí.paále*	'calabash'
utu.máshu	'a few words'	<	*amá.shu*	'words'
útw.aakúlya	'delicious foods'; 'variety of small foods'	<	*ích.aakúlya*	'food'
aka.búyo	'good place' 'small place'	<	*ubú.yo*	'place'
aka.yúumba	'hut' 'beautiful house'	<	*iny'.úumba*	'house'

❖ Pronouns

• Personal pronouns

  • Subject pronouns

Independent subject pronouns are of two types: emphatic and copular. The former are typically used to focus or emphasize the participant. The latter equate a participant and a characteristic.

  • Emphatic

	Singular	Plural
1	*úne*	*útwe*
2	*ú(g)we, úwe*	*úmwe*
3	*úmweéne*	*ábeéne*

úne niinong'ónaga ukuti pakóócha
'(as for) me, I was thinking that it's hot'

útwe ákaaya kíitu kaa kuTaanzanía
'(as for) us, our home is in Tanzania'

úwe upaashikisháange ngaáni
'(as for) you, you should be very worried'

  • Copular

	Singular	Plural
1	*née*	*twée*
2	*wée*	*mwée*

3	Cl		Cl	
	1	*wii*	*2*	*boo*
	3	*goo*	*4*	*yoo*
	5	*lyoo*	*6*	*goo*
	7	*choo*	*8*	*fyoo*
	9	*yoo*	*10*	*shoo*
	11	*lwoo*	see 10	
	12	*koo*	*13*	*twoo*
	14	*bwoo*	see 6	
	16	*poo*		
	17	*koo*		
	18	*mwoo*		

31

uMwaandemele wíi kátoote 'Mwandemele is a first-born child'

páapo akáfwa uné mwoo née munáandi léka
'when she died, me, at that time, I was very small'

kúkaaya kóo ílyiita koo kwlpóónjola
'in the village whose name is Iponjola'

búubo bugiindikiwe íngaáni choo chipúumu
'the one [beer] which is very popular is *chipumu*'

• Object pronouns

Object pronouns are like their subject counterparts. They are only used as oblique objects, i.e., as objects of *ná-* 'with' and the linking connector *-aa*.

	Singular		Plural	
1	*úne*		*útwe*	
2	*úgwe, úwe*		*úmwe*	
3	Cl		Cl	
	1	*(g)we*	*2*	*bo*
	3	*go*	*4*	*yo*
	5	*lyo*	*6*	*go*
	7	*cho*	*8*	*fyo*
	9	*yo*	*10*	*sho*
	11	*lwo*	*see 10*	
	12	*ko*	*13*	*two*
	14	*bwo*	*see 6*	
	16	*po*		
	17	*k(w)o*		
	18	*mwo*		

úmukolo aapulíkana nágwe
'the young woman has agreed with him'

bakiitiláashe pakuny'atula ukuyá nábwo kumúliisha kúkwaábo
'they just invited [others] to carry (and go) with it [flour] to the home of the man'

akeendáá nácho iisíla yaa mumatípa áye muChíbula
'he used to walk with it [food] on the dirt road going to Chibula'

*kwaandá tááshi ulóonde umúliindu yóo kubá **nágwe** pachikóole*
'you first look for a young woman with whom you become steady
[LIT who you be with her at engagement]'

*luumbá kwaa **úne*** 'face (toward) me'

*áálí n'ubúng'waamu bwaa **úne*** 'she was pregnant with me'

- Reflexive pronouns

Reflexive pronouns, in general, incorporate the root *-eene* 'self' plus the appropriate class prefix. First person pronouns, however, appear to be derived from reduplication of the basic pronoun with lengthening of the first vowel: *ne + ne, twe + twe.*

	Singular		Plural	
1	*néene*		*twéetwe*	
2	*úweéne*		*ábeéne*	
3	Cl		Cl	
	1	*úmweéne*	*2*	*ábeéne*
	3	*ú(g)weéne*	*4*	*íyeéne*
	5	*ílyeéne*	*6*	*ágeéne*
	7	*ícheéne*	*8*	*ífyeéne*
	9	*íyeéne*	*10*	*ísheéne*
	11	*úlweéne*	see *10*	
	12	*ákeéne*	*13*	*útweéne*
	14	*úbweéne*	see *6*	

*imbúuke **néene** né waa pamupáando*
'I should go myself, I, the chair'

***úmwééne** páapo akafwáanga, akabaleka ábaana báake biingíbíingííshe*
'when he, himself, died, he left behind just his many, many children'

*aboosékulu **ábeéne** bakakweeny'aga úmweenda mulufúkwe*
'our grandparents, themselves, used to wrap the cloth around the stomach'

*ípelekete yikuyaanááshe n'ipenéenga lóole **ákeéne** kakuba kanáandi*
'the *ipelekete* drum looks just like the *ipenenga* drum, but itself it is small(er)'

33

oneself

	Singular	Plural
1	*nemwenééko*	*twemwenééko*
2	*wemwenééko*	*mwemwenééko*

by oneself

	Singular	Plural
1	*nímweene*	*twíbeene*
2	*wímweene*	*mwíbeene*

liingá wiiganíte kumogagá wímwééne
'if you want, you dance by yourself'

• Reciprocal pronouns

The independent reciprocal pronouns are formed with the stem *-eené–ééne*, prefixing the appropriate C- agreement prefix.

*báanda ukulwakulwá piipípíípi **beenébééne***
'they began to fight frequently [with] one another'

*bakatíí biitilanité **beenébééne** pakubega amaléshi*
'they had invited each other to harvest millet'

• Possessive pronouns

Possessive pronouns are formed by affixing the appropriate agreement prefix to the possessive stem (*-aa* + ROOT). Simple pronominal possessives require a VC- agreement prefix, i.e., one including the augment vowel, whereas copular pronominal possessives affix only the C- agreement prefix. The tone patterns for the two types also differ, the former having two high tones, the latter one.

• Simple pronominal possessives

	Singular	Plural
1	V́C-*aángu*	V́C-*iítu*
2	V́C-*aáko*	V́C-*iíny'u*
3	V́C-*aáke*	V́C-*aábo*

úwaángu akabá wiisóongo kubáníne bóoshi
'mine [father] was the oldest of all of them'

34

*leembá n'úuwe pipéépala **ílyaáko***
'write, you too, on that paper [of] yours'

*wéeshi akuloonda uyu **íyaáke** uyu **íyaáke***
'each looks for his own [cow]'

*akuboombááshe **íshaáke*** 'she is just doing hers [work]'

*akabweelá nátwo, **ákaáke** n'ákaa Símwaáyi*
'he went home with them, his and Simwayi's'

- Copular pronominal possessives

	Singular	Plural
1	C-*áángu*	C-*íítu*
2	C-*ááko*	C-*ííny'u*
3	C-*ááke*	C-*áábo*

*ubuny'afyáale **bwáángu*** 'the chieftaincy is mine'

*imbóombo yaa kukeetakeeta ífyaa pálapala pipenéenga **yáábo***
'the task of taking care of things there at the *ipenenga* dance is theirs
[old men]'

- Relative pronouns

Relative pronouns are formed by affixing the appropriate agreement prefix to
the root *-ée* for personal participants, or *-óo* for third person.

- Simple relative pronoun: 'who/which/that'

	Singular	Plural
1	*née*	*twée*
2	*wée*	*mwée*

	Cl		Cl	
3	*1*	*yóo*	*2*	*bóo*
	3	*góo*	*4*	*yóo*
	5	*lyóo*	*6*	*góo*
	7	*chóo*	*8*	*fyóo*
	9	*yóo*	*10*	*shóo*
	11	*lwóo*	*see 10*	
	12	*kóo*	*13*	*twóo*
	14	*bwóo*	*see 6*	

16	póo
17	kwóo
18	mwóo

úmukolo aamukóleka chóo alí nácho.
'the woman hands him what she has'

aakúula ílyiino lyóo lyaamubábaga.
's/he has removed the tooth that was hurting her'

• Indefinite relative pronoun: 'the one(s)/way/time who/which/that'

	Singular	Plural
1	*néene*	*twéetwe*
2	*wéewe*	*mwéemwe*

3	Cl		Cl	
	1	*yúuyo*	*2*	*báabo*
	3	*gúugo*	*4*	*yíiyo*
	5	*líilyo*	*6*	*gáago*
	7	*chíicho*	*8*	*fíifyo*
	9	*yíiyo*	*10*	*shíisho*
	11	*lúulwo*	*see 10*	
	12	*káako*	*13*	*túutwo*
	14	*búubwo*	*see 6*	
	16	*páapo*		
	17	*kúukwo*		
	18	*múumwo*		

umúliisha yúuyo ateegíte tukuti umukéenja.
'a man who is not married is called a bachelor'

twéetwe *twaayúga léka*
'we are the ones who were complaining [= speaking a lot]'

36

• Copular relative pronoun: 'is/are who/which/that'

	Singular	Plural
1	*nenée*	*twetwée*
2	*wewée*	*mwemwée*

3	Cl		Cl	
	1	*(g)wéeyo*	*2*	*bóobo*
	3	*góogo*	*4*	*yóoyo*
	5	*lyóolyo*	*6*	*góogo*
	7	*chóocho*	*8*	*fyóofyo*
	9	*yóoyo*	*10*	*shóosho*
	11	*lwóolwo*	*see 10*	
	12	*kóoko*	*13*	*twóotwo*
	14	*bwóobwo*	*see 6*	
	16	*póopo*		
	17	*kwóokwo*		
	18	*mwúumwc*		

Íifumu lyóolyo likumalila pakubabuula.
'the chief is he who speaks last'

yóoyo yikututuula kúno ukufwaaná n'ubumany'íli.
'it is what helps us here with resepct to education'

kookuti wéeyo aamu\úsala ukubá múlume.
'it means it is he whom she has chosen to be her husband'

útukuku túútwo twóotwo twaapaapiwe mumasuba.
'those chicks are the ones which were born yesterday'

• Copular indefinite relative pronoun: 'is/are the one/s who/which/that'

	Singular	Plural
1	*néene*	*twéetwe*
2	*wéewe*	*mwéemwe*

3	Cl		Cl	
	1	weyúuyo	2	bobáabo
	3	gogúugo	4	yoyíiyo
	5	lyolíilyo	6	gogáago
	7	chochíicho	8	fyofyíifyo
	9	yoyíiiyo	10	shoshíisho
	11	lwolúulwo	see 1 0	
	12	kokáako	13	twotúutwo
	14	bwobúubwc	see 6	
	16	popáapo		
	17	kokúuko		
	18	mwomúumv		

umúfuusha **weyúuyo** *akwaanda ukuyugha kwaa ng'ína waa múliindu*
'the boy's marriage representative is the one who begins speaking to
the girl's mother'

mwomúumwo *íny'éégá yikweendela múkaaya kíitu*
'it is how [the way in which] a marriage is done in our village'

• Demonstrative copular relative pronoun:
  'that/those is/are who/which/that'

3	Cl		Cl	
	1	yúyúuyo	2	bábáabo
	3	gúgúugo	4	yíyííyo
	5	líliílyo	6	gágáago
	7	chíchíicho	8	fífíifyo
	9	yíyííyo	10	shíshíisho
	11	lúlúulwo	see 10	
	12	kákáako	13	túutúutwo
	14	búbúubwo	see 6	
	16	pápáapo		
	17	kúkúuko		
	18	múmúumwc		

*poo íishiku **lílíílyo** bakuti poo pachíingi*
'so, that day is what they call "pachingi"'

*ulusélo **lúlúúlwo** lúpya*
'that winnowing basket is that [one] which is new'

PART 3

NOUN MODIFICATION

❖ Agreement

All noun modifiers and verbs indicate agreement with the head noun through affixation of an agreement prefix. The form of the agreement prefix attached to the modifier or verb differs for each noun class. There are three general patterns, as shown in Table 3.1. Prefixes (and the corresponding augment) are identified by numbers that index the appropriate forms.

Table 3.1 Agreement Patterns

CLASS	ADJ	LNK	AGR	
1/1a	*(u)mu-*	*(u)w-*	*yu-*	*a-*
2/2a	*(a)ba-*	*(a)ba-*	*ba-*	
3	*(u)mu-*	*(u)w-*	*gu-*	
4	*(i)mi-*	*(i)y-*	*yi-*	
5/5a	*(i)li-, ii-*	*(i)ly-*	*li-*	
6	*(a)ma-*	*(a)g-*	*ga-*	
7	*(i)chi-*	*(i)ch-*	*chi-*	
8	*(i)fi-*	*(i)fy-*	*fi-*	
9	*(i)n-*	*(i)y-*	*yi-*	
10	*(i)n-*	*(i)sh-*	*shi-*	
11	*(u)lu-*	*(u)lw-*	*lu-*	
12	*(a)ka-*	*(a)k-*	*ka-*	
13	*(u)tu-*	*(u)tw-*	*tu-*	
14	*(u)bu-*	*(u)bw-*	*bu-*	
15	*(u)ku-*	*(u)kw-*	*ku-*	
16	*pa-*	*p-*	*pa-*	
17	*ku-*	*kw-*	*ku-*	
18	*mu-*	*mw-*	*mu-*	

ADJ: adjectives, colors, numbers (other than one), *-iingi* 'many', *-naandi* 'few', *-nine* 'other [same]'

LNK: possessives, connective linker *-aa*

AGR: (i) demonstratives, *-mu–eene* 'one', *-eene* 'only', *-mo/-mu* 'certain, some', *-ooshi* 'all', *-liinga* 'how many, how much', *-ngi* 'other'

      (ii) verbs, *-liku* 'which (interrogative)'

      cl. 1: (i) *yu-*; (ii) *a-*

43

❖ Connective linker *-aa*

The linking element *-aa* connects two nouns in a so-called genitive relation. The nouns may be common nouns, or one may be a nominal infinitive of class 15. In each case, different kinds of relations may be expressed. The linker typically requires agreement with the head noun. However, in a locative use, it occurs invariably as *kwaa*.

- Linking noun and noun

  - possessive relation

    úbubine bwaa múundu 'a person's illness'

    umúnuusi waa ny'áma 'an animal's scent'

    abapáapi bóoshi baa mulumyáana 'all parents of the young man'

    ábakashi baa bánine 'others' wives'

    íimbuno yaa ingulúbe 'a pig's nose'

    umulómu waá njeeye 'a crab's mouth'

    abénéécho baa ndéege 'plane's owners'

    ubútuukifu bwaa kámu 'the warmth of the sunlight'

    kuumbénu kwaa cháálichi 'in back of the church'

  - descriptive relation

    iiny'áma yaa ngulúbe 'pork' [LIT. meat of pig]

    ílyaani lyaa líkoondo 'yam leaf' [LIT. leaf of yam plant]

    imbóoto yaa bugáli 'bugali pot' [N.B. not 'pot of bugali']

    ubúyo bwaa mbúungo 'funeral site'

    úbutolwe bwaa lúko úlu 'a problem of this kind'

    ichóongo cháá kalulu 'the noise of ululations'

    úmukolo waa pabúng'waamu 'pregnant woman'

    [LIT. woman of at heaviness]

  - appositive relation

    ibóoma lyaa Chitípa 'the district of Chitipa'

    áali n'ubúng'waamu bwaa úne 'she was pregnant with me'

    [LIT was with the heaviness of me]

  - goal relation

    úmweenda waa ng'ína 'cloth for her mother'

    indaláma shaa boowísekulu 'money for his grandfathers'

- source relation

    abáníne ábaa kuChiíkuumbulu 'others from Chikumbulu'

    iny'óóndo íyaa muny'áma yáa nguku 'chicken gizzard'

                            [LIT. gizzard of in meat of chicken]

- partitive or measurement relation

    akapúúsa kaa ny'áma 'a small piece of meat'

    ichiluundílo chaa báandu 'a group of people'

- Linking infinitive and noun

  - subjective relation

    ukubabá kwaa (lí)puumba 'the pain of a boil'

                [the boil hurts]

    ukulilá kwaa chigáayo 'the sound of a grinding mill'

                [the mill produces a sound]

    ukumuutá kwaa ng'óombe 'the mooing of cattle'

                [the cattle moo]

  - objective relation

    ukushiilá kwáabo kwaa múundu

    'their [way of] burying of a person'

  - manner relation

    ukwiimbá kwaa lusekélo 'joyous singing'

  - instrumental relation

    ámiishi gaa kupííyíla 'water for cooking'

    ímyeenda yaa kumógela 'clothes for dancing'

  - purposive relation

    ubúyo bwaa kuliisháámwo ing'óombe

    'a place for grazing cattle at'

    iny'úumba yaa kupiiyáámwo 'a house for cooking in'

  - descriptive relation

    úmukolo waa kuyáana 'a suitable woman'

    úbuumi bwaa kutámiwa 'a life of hardship'

    ichilóonda chaa kulumiwá n'íinjoka 'a snakebite wound'

    akabalílo kaa kweeganílana 'a time for marriage'

    ifíindu fyaa kugulísha 'things for selling'

    imbúungo shaa kupaambanapáámbana

    'different kinds of diseases'

• Linker agreement incorporating an augment

Although the linker -aa invariably requires agreement marking, it varies as to whether or not it affixes an augment. It has not yet been possible to identify what factors determine choice of one form over the other. Several pairs of comparable constructions, differing in use of the augment [in bold], are provided below. Miscellaneous examples follow.

> *ichi.boombélo chaa muny'úumba* 'household utensil'
> *ichí.lílo íchaa muny'úumba* 'household container'
>
> *akápaango kaa báándali* 'the story of the Ndali people'
> *akápaango ákaa lúko lwíitu* 'the story of our clan'
>
> *amapúushi gaa maléshi* 'millet stalks'
> *ubugáli úbwaa fílóómbe* 'maize bugali'
>
> *íny'iimbo shaa kupaambanapáámbana* 'songs of different kinds'
> *utusúmo útwaa kulekanalékana* 'dances of various kinds'

• miscellaneous examples

> *íishiku ílyaa níngeelo* 'the next day'
>
> *múny'aambi yáake íyaa paany'úma* 'in his back pocket'
>
> *iny'úumba íyaáke íyaa kúgona* 'his own house for sleeping'
>
> *bakabegaga amákwaamba ágaa fitíindi n'amásakata gaa
> kumuteengeláápo úmwaana n'uung'ína*
> 'they used to take the bark and dry leaves of banana trees
> to lay under the child and mother'
>
> *ámashiku manáandííshe ágaa bwaandílo*
> 'just a few days at the beginning'

• Locative or directional relation: *kwaa*

A locative, directional, or ownership relation is expressed by use of the class 17 locative prefix affixed to the -aa linker.

> *-iikalá kwaa Luséba* 'live at Luseba'
>
> *-fumá kwaa Mwaamúkuumbwa* 'come from Mwamukumbwa'
>
> *-aashima ibúuku kwaa Lusékelo* 'borrow a book from Lusekelo'
>
> *-yiilá kwaa Túúnduma* 'go through Tuunduma'
>
> *-buuká kwaa malafyáale* 'go to the chief'
>
> *-eega mupáka kwaa Máfiinga* 'take [s.o.] up to Mafinga'
>
> *-tabula indaláma kwaa Lusáayo* 'pay back money to Lusayo'
>
> *-luumba kwaa úne* 'face [toward] me'
>
> *-yá kwaa Tíiti* 'go to Titi's place'

46

❖ Demonstratives

There are ten lexical patterns for forming demonstratives in Chindali and four roots associated with these patterns: Ø, -o, -la, -laa, as in Table 3.2. Two are used specifically in discourse, one only in spatial reference. The templatic segmental material is determined by the CV–substance of the noun class prefix except for those noun prefixes that include a nasal. In the latter cases, the C of the template is invariably [y] for classes 1 (umu-), 4 (imi-), and 9 (iN-), [ɣ] for classes 3 (umu-) and 6 (ama-), and [ʃ] for class 10 (in-).

Table 3.2 Templates for demonstratives

	Neutral			Emphatic
Proxi-mate	CV́-V that mentioned	V́-CV this	CV́-V́-CV this right here	CV́-CV-V́-CV this very one here
		V́-C(G)-o that/the afore-mentioned	CV́-V́-C(G)-o that already mentioned	CV́-CV-V́-C(G)-o that very one
Distant	CV́-la CV́-la that one knows	CV́-la that yonder		
		CV́-laa that way over there		

[Forms used only in discourse reference are listed within the box in bold outline; the form enclosed in double lines is used only in spatial reference.]

pakabalílo áka 'at this time'

úmweenda úgo 'that [aforementioned] cloth'

pachishíbá chííchi 'at this very same pool'

ichíinja chíchííchi 'this very year'

umugúunda gúugo that field [mentioned earlier]'

abáandu baa múkaaya múla múla bábili ába
'these two people of that village [one knows]'

indéege yíla 'that plane yonder'

úbutolwe bwáá miishi úbu 'this problem of water'

47

The demonstrative typically follows its head noun. However, it may also precede the head noun, although this appears to be uncommon.

tukweegá fíla fíla ífipapa
'we take those animal hides [that we know from context]'

❖ Adjectives

Unlike many Bantu languages, Chindali has many adjectives. There is a large set of inherent adjectives (Tables 3.3 - 3.7), as well as a productive means for deriving adjectives from verbs (Table 3.8). Adjectives follow the noun they modify and require agreement with it.

Table 3.3 Attributes of sex, age, size, and weight

-kolo	'female'	*-liisha*	'male'
-deende	'hen'		
-pya	'new'		
-fyeele	'newborn'		
-keke	'young'	*-kuulu*	'very old'
-naandi	'small, young'	*-kulu*	'big'
-piimba	'short'	*-tali*	'long, tall'
-pese	'thin'	*-ng'wame*	'heavy'
		-shito	'heavy'

Table 3.4 Attributes of quality or form

-iisa	'good'	*-biibi*	'bad'
-komu	'good'		
-pepe	'easy'	*-pala*	'difficult'
-toofu	'soft'	*-kafu*	'hard'
-ny'afu	'tasty'	*-bisi*	'unripe'
-sheenga	'round'	*-kole*	'sharp'
-fukamu	'bowl-shaped'	*-uubi*	'sharp'
		-fuluumbi	'dusty'

Table 3.5 Attributes of human behavior or characteristics

-ooloolo	'polite'	-beeshi	'restless'
-shisha	'serious'	-guumba	'sterile'
-yebeshi	'clever'	-kali	'fierce'
		-kata	'lazy'
		-pafu	'greedy'
		-piina	'poor'

Table 3.6 Miscellaneous adjectives

-kale	'long ago'	-puuma	'whole'
-luulu	'particular'	-salaanje	'engraved'
-palapala	'exhibiting trait to an	extreme'	

Table 3.7 Colors

-eelu(fu)	'white'
-sweepu	'white'
-tiitu	'black'
-kesamu	'red'
-buufu	'blue'

Table 3.8 Adjectives derived from verbs

-kabi	'wealthy'	<	-kaba	'gain by doing sth'
-ny'ali	'dirty'	<	-ny'ala	'become dirty'
-buluunge	'round'	<	-buluunga	'make round'
-che	'sharp'	<	-cha	'be sharp'
-gaande	'thin'	<	-gaanda	'become thin'
-gome	'mature'	<	-goma	'become old'
-hoboke	'happy	<	-hoboka	'be happy'
-iisule	'swollen'	<	-iisula	'swell'
-kaangale	'old'	<	-kaangala	'grow old'
-pyooke	'broken'	<	-pyooka	'break'
-sekele	'friendly'	<	-sekela	'be happy'
-shiinge	'charmed'	<	-shiinga	'protect by charm'
-suupe	'dull, blunt'	<	-suupa	'become blunt'

-tone	'curdled'	<	-tona	'be ripe'
-bofu	'rotten'	<	-bola	'rot'
-kafu	'hard'	<	-kala	'harden'
-golofu	'straight'	<	-golola	'straighten'
-galamu	'flat'	<	-galama	'lie on back'
-uumu	'dry'	<	-uuma	'be dry'

❖ **Quantifying determiners**

The quantifying determiners can be divide into two groups: those that form their agreement following the pattern typical of adjectives, and those that form agreement typical of determiners [see Table 3.1].

Agreement type: ADJECTIVAL   DETERMINER

-naandi 'few'   -mu, -mo 'some'

-iingi 'many'   -ooshi 'all'

-nine 'other [same]'   -ngi 'other [different]'

-eene 'only'

-naandi   'few, a few, a bit'

góope amasitóolo manáandi nalóoli 'also, stores are very few'

ámashiku manáandíishe 'just a few days'

utwookóofi tunáandi 'a little bit of coffee'

-iingi   'many; much'

mumabúyo ámiingi 'in many places'

ing'óombe íny'iingi 'many cattle'

amagáli ámiingi 'much mush'

ifitékiwa ífyaa kulekanalékana ífyiingi
'livestock of many different kinds'

-nine   '(an)other [of the same kind]'

n'ifíindu ifínine ífyiingi léka
'and a lot of other things'

liingá wéepe yulá iimite pakáti áálita abánine bakumupokéela
'if, too, that one who is standing in the middle gets tired, others take her place'

útááta wáangu ali pa Ipóónjola; umúnine akáfwa
'my father is at Iponjola; another died'

-ngi   '(an)other [of a different kind]'

iiny'áma iyíingi 'any other type of meat'

bakabáámwo ábáá fikolo ifíingi
'there were those of other clans there'

bakuti úkiise sóóna íishiku ilíingi
'they say you should come again another day'

uyúungi yúuo chaamuny'ámula akuny'amukaga pakwiityóonga
'anyone else who is carried away [by the singing] gets up and dances'

-éene   'only; alone'

akukomaaná tááshi n'uung'ína wáá mukolo mwéene
'he first meets with her mother only'

ubúpaambane buli páanjuga péene
'the difference is in the language only'

akapaapa ábaana bábili abalumyáana béene
'he fathered only two male children'

shímo bakupiiya pamúpééne n'índuuny'e, shímo shéene
'some [meats] they cook together with bananas, some alone'

	Singular noun	Plural noun
-éeshi *-óoshi*	'each; any(one), (any)thing; whole'	'every(one), every(thing); all'

	Singular	Plural
1	—	*twéeshi*
2	—	*mwéeshi*
3	*wéeshi*	*bóoshi*

tukwoongaanááshe pakumogá pamúpééne twéeshi
'we just mix together when dancing, all of us'

mwéeshi mwííteendekeshe ukwaanda
'all of you should be ready to begin'

wéeshi akufwaalá móo iiganííle 'each dresses the way s/he likes'

wéeshi yóo íisa pambúungo akubá n'úbwiigane bwaa kubiikáápo kámu
'anyone who has come to the funeral has the pleasure of giving something'

uMaláawi wéeshi 'the whole of Malawi'

bóoshi bábili ába 'both of them'

Cl		Cl	
1	*wéeshi*	2	*bóoshi*
3	*góoshi*	4	*yóoshi*
5	*lyóoshi*	6	*góoshi*
7	*chóoshi*	8	*fyóoshi*
9	*yóoshi*	10	*shóoshi*
11	*lwóoshi*	see	10
12	*kóoshi*	13	*twóoshi*
14	*bwóoshi*	see	6
16	*póoshi*		
17	*kóoshi*		
18	*mwóoshi*		

ichiluundílo chóoshi íchaa finy'ámáana
'the whole gathering of animals'

tukuyileká yóoshi imíindu pála pála
'we leave the whole mess right there'

úbushiku bwóoshi 'the whole night'

póoshi pámwaany'a pííbwe 'all over the top of the rock'

imbíingu yikapatiinganyá shóoshi íny'oobe
'handcuffs bound both hands'

mukupulikaná fyóoshi ukufwaaná na fyóo bakuloonda
'you negotiate everything according to what they want'

-mo ~ -mu   'some, certain'

This stem alternates in form depending on the vowel of the prefix. The form *-mu* occurs following prefixal [a], the form *-mo* elsewhere.

abáandu bámu bábili 'a certain two people'

kuloonda umúundu yúmo, umumany'áani wáako
'you look for a certain person, your friend'

filikó fímo ifiyúni fyóo fikwiisa múchishiku
'there are certain birds that come during the rainy season'

liingááshe chímo chíingila muny'úumba yáake akusáámaga
'if something just gets inside its house, it moves'

naa-AGR-mo '(not) anything/anybody; nothing/nobody'

The negative counterpart is constructed by prefixing *naa-* to the affirmative form. With a negative marker on the verb, the sense is 'not any(thing/body)'; without the negative marker, it is 'nothing/nobody'.

> *abáliisha batákweegá naakámu* 'men do not take anything'
>
> *tutákubá n'ínoongwa naayímo* 'we do not have any guilt'
>
> *táabátwaage utusúmo naatúmo naatúmo utú nguliingaanya pánu*
> 'they will not find at all any of these dances I am describing here'
>
> *pakabalílo áka naachímo naachímo chikuboombíwa*
> 'at this time, nothing at all happens'

❖ Comparatives and superlatives

In comparative constructions, the proposition expressed in the matin clause is compared with that expressed in the subordinate clause. The relationship of the nouns via the standard of comparison may be equational or differentiating.

• Comparatives

  • Equational

Equational comparison is indicated in one of two ways: (i) by use of the conjunction *ngáti* 'like', or (ii) by use of the verb *-gelela* 'be equal, similar'. The standard of comparison may be expressed by either a noun or a verb with *ngáti*, only by a noun with *-gelela*.

(i) use of *ngáti* 'like'

> *uLusáayo alí   n'amáka   **ngáti** uKapáamba*
>   3S.be with.strength
> 'Lusayo is as strong as Kapamba'

> *uNjéeki asekiilé   **ngáti** uLusekélo*
>   3S.be_happy.CMPL
> 'Njeki is as happy as Lusekelo'

> *uBúpe akuboombá **ngáti** mwóo uMáake akubóómbela*
>   3S.PR.work like   how   3S.PR.work.APPL
> 'Bupe works as much as Make works'

> *poopé shitákahoboshaangá **ngáti** shíisho bakiimbaa ábaachipáanga*
> 'even then, they [songs] were not as interesting as those which
> church-goers sang'

53

(ii) use of *-gelela* 'be equal, similar'

> *uLusáayo **ageliilééshe***   *úbutali n'uKapáamba*
>   3S.be_equal.CMPL.just height   with.K
> 'Lusayo is as tall as Kapamba'

> *uLusáayo n'uKapáamba **bageliilééshe***   *úbutali*
>   and   3P.be_equal.CMPL height
> 'Lusayo is as tall as Kapamba'

- Differentiating

Differentiating comparisons may indicate either a greater or lesser relationship between two entities in terms of some attribute. In such cases, either the verbal noun *ukukiinda* 'surpass' or *ukupoota* 'defeat' is employed.

(i) Greater than

> *uLusáayo mútali*   ***ukukiinda** uKapáamba*
>   3S.COP.tall surpass
> 'Lusayo is taller than Kapamba'

> *uNjéeki asekiile*   ***ukukiinda** uLusekélo*
>   3S.be_happy.CMPL surpass
> 'Njeki is happier than Lusekelo'

> *abáandu ábiingi bakulima*   *índuuny'e **ukukiinda** ifíloómbe*
> 2.people   2.many   2.CC.cultivate bananas   surpass   maize
> 'more people cultivate bananas than maize'

> *ákasumo áka*   *kakuhobosha*   *panáandi **ukukiinda** akáníne*
> 12.dance   12.this 12.PR.be_interesting 16.little   surpass   12.other
> 'this dance is a little more interesting than the other one'

> *mwoo báaga ukuti áanda ukulimá lúkulu nápa**kupoota** abáníne,*
> *báanda pakubapoka ífyiisi*
> 'when they found that he began to cultivate a lot, even more than others, they began to take fields by force'

(ii) Lesser than

> *uKapáamba alí*   *n'amáka*   *manáandi **ukukiinda** uLusáayo*
>   3S.BE with.12.strength 12.little   surpass
> 'Kapamba is less strong than Lusayo'

> *ukuposolá*   *kwáake kupépéépo **ukupootá** yúuyo*   *amupiile*
> 15.pay_damages its   15.easy.bit surpass   that.one 3S.3S.give.CMPL
>
>   *ulufúkwe*
>   belly
>
> 'its indemnity payment is less than that for one who has impregnated [a woman]'

• Superlatives

Superlatives may be indicated in at least three ways. Like differentiating comparisons, they may employ the verbal noun *ukukiinda* 'surpass', in which case the relationship is expressed with respect to *-óoshi* 'all'. Rather than *ukukiinda*, the verb *-poota* 'defeat' may be used, or the locative prefix *ku-* may be cliticized to the noun phrase.

> *uLusáayo alí n'amáka **uku-kiindá bóoshi***
> 'Lusayo is the strongest of all'

> *akabá n'amahála **a-ka-poot-á bóoshi***
> 'he was more intelligent than anybody'

> *apá baakwáá Njebéte bóo **ba-ku-poot-a** uku-líma amálíma*
> 'now, it is those from Njebete who grow the most beans'

> *útaáta úwaángu akabá wiisóongo **ku-bá-níne bóoshi***
> 'my father was the oldest of all the others'   [or *ku-bóoshi*]

If the sense implies an excessive or exaggerated amount of the attribute, then the adverb *lukúlu* 'too much' is employed

> *uKapáamba alí n'amahálá lúkulu*
> 'Kapamba is the smartest/too smart'

> *uAambíile akukiindá lubilolubíló lúkulu*
> 'Ambile runs the fastest/too fast'

❖ **Numbers**

The numerical system of Chindali appears to have shifted from a tradi-tional system, in which the first five numerals required agreement with the noun and the second five occurred in apposition to the noun, to a quinary system in which the numerals from six to nine are constructed on *-haano* 'five'. While some older speakers may still use the traditional system, younger speakers have shifted. With the introduction of English in school, many younger speakers have begun using English borrowings from four to ten.

• Cardinal

> *ichíinja chimúchééne* 'one year'
> *ábaana baháano na yúmo* 'six children'
> *amakóópala ilóongo na limúlyeéne* 'eleven cents'
> *indaláma myáa yibili* 'two hundred kwacha'

55

	Traditional	Recent shifts	English borrowings		
1	-mú–eéne		wáanu	11	ilóongo na -mú–eéne
2	-bili		túu	12	ilóongo na -bili
3	-tatu		filíi	13	ilóongo na -tatu
4	-náayi		fóolo		
5	-háano		fáyifi		
6	ntaandátu	-háano na -mo	síkisi		
7	?	-háano na -bili	sébeni	20	malóongo mábili
8	lwéele	-háano na -tatu	éiti	30	malóongo mátatu
9	?	-háano na -na	náyini		
10	kaloongo		téeni	100	myáa
				200	myáa yíbili

• Ordinal

Ordinal numbers are either in class 14 (*ubu-*) or class 7 (*ichi-*). All but first and last use the same stem as the cardinal numbers. First and last differ in that the stem is derived from a verb, *-aandila* 'begin' and *-malila* 'finish', respectively. An ordinal is expressed in a linking construction with the connective linker *-aa*.

First	ubwaandílo	
2nd	úbubili	ichibíili
3rd	úbutatu	ichitatu
4th	ubúna, ubunáayi	ubunáayi
Last	ubumalílo	

íishiku ílyaa bwaandílo 'the first day'

umútu gwáá bubili the second topic'

úmukashi wáá butatu 'the third wife'

usabáata úwaa bunáayi 'the fourth week'

amáshu gáake gaa bumalílo 'her last words'

❖ **Interrogatives**

Interrogatives are expressed either as independent in-situ words or by suffixes on the verb.

buléele	'how'	*ichíisu pakále chikabá buléele?'*
		'the world a long time ago was how?'
		ukukitá buléele? 'you do this how?'
kútali buléele	'how far'	*ínga ku améélikáá kúuko, kútali buléele?*
		'so then, to America there, it is how far?'
chóoni	'what'	*tubóombe chóoni?* 'what should we do?'
or		
kóoni	'what'	*tulí na kóoni pákaaya pánu?*
		'we have what in this house here?'
káliinga	'how often'	*uungapulíkila káliínga ífyaa muny'úumba?*
		'you can follow how often parent's advice
		[LIT. things of the house]?'
kúugu	'where'	*shááfuma kúugu shímo?*
		'it [money] came from where, some of it?'
líigi	'when'	*bakany'amuka líigi?* 'they left when?'
chóoni chóo	'why'	*chóoni chóo mwiganité léka pakumoga*
(see also *-ki* below)		*umwiinóoge?*
		'why do you like so much performing the
		umwinoge dance?'
-íini	'who'	*wée wíini?* 'you are who?'
-áani	'whose'	*ichíloómbe íchi cháani?*
		'this ear of corn is whose?'
-ki	'what'	*ngímba tukóóshéeki?* 'what should we do?'
		ngímba ifígaamba n'ímishitu fikwaagibwá
		kwóoki?
		'the mountains and forests are found
		at what place?'
	'why'	*ngímba mááyi kóo waakiindílaga*
		waakiindílagáaki?
		'madam, why were you running away to
		where you were running to?'
		chifúukwa chiki 'the reason is what'?
		(= 'why'?)

-liku	'which'	*úmulume wáako wee áliku?*
		'your husband is which one?'
		néege chíliku íchaakuti imbíiye ólo índye
		'I should take which thing such that
		I cook or eat [it]?'
-liinga	'how many'	*ulí n'ing'óombe shíliinga?*
		'how many head of cattle do you have?'
	'how much'	*wáákaba shíliínga?*
		'how much profit have you made?'

PART 4

VERBS:
STRUCTURE AND MORPHOLOGY

❖ Structure of the verbal word

Typical of Bantu languages, Chindali is an agglutinating language. The verbal word, consequently, consists of multiple grammatical categories, only three of which—subject prefix (SP), Base, and inflection final suffix (F)—are obligatorily marked. The basic organizational pattern of these categories is as follows, obligatory elements in bold, optional in plain text.

• Finite word-form: General categorial template

BASE = RAD + EXT

Prefixal elements: Fut = **SP** – TMP – OM/*ii* – **BASE** –

Suffixal elements: – **BASE** – ASP_1 – Vox – ASP_2 – **F** – Asp_3 = PoF

Fut	future
SP	subject prefix [see Person/number marking, §x]
TMP	tempus: tense, tenor, event modality
OM	object marker [see Person/number marking, §x]
ii	reflexive marker and middle voice
RAD	verb radical
Ext	verb extensions
Asp	aspect
Vox	voice changing suffixes: causative and passive
F	inflection final suffix
PoF	post-final clitics: locative and partitive
	miscellaneous (e.g., *-she* 'just' and *-nga* 'only')

Each of these categories is discussed in more detail in following sections.

General structural relations

MACRO-STEM
◆————————————————————————◆
STEM
◆——————————————————————◆
BASE
◆———————◆
– OM – RAD – EXT – ASP – Vox – ASP – F – ASP = PoF

• Substantival word-form: infinitives

uku – *ii*/OM – **RAD** – Ext – *a* = PoF

61

❖ The verb radical

The radical comprises the semantic core of the verbal word; that is, it embodies the minimal morphological material that provides the basic meaning of the verb. There are three types: (1) those verbs composed of a simple root, (2) those comprising a root plus lexicalized expansion, and (3) those comprising a reduplicand plus its root (and potential expansion). An expansion is a formally segmentable element attached to a root that never occurs in the language without it (but cf. Schadeberg 2003 for a slightly different use). Unlike extensional suffixes, expansions form an integral part of the radical and must be reduplicated. Extensional suffixes are optionally reduplicated. Although radicals can often be decomposed into a root and expansion, or into a partial reduplicand plus root, they are completely lexicalized and do not represent productive derivations.

RADICAL

Redup . ROOT . Expansion

❖ The simple root

The canonical form of the verb root in Chindali, as in most Bantu languages, is -CV(:)C-. Vowel length is distinctive, so there is a short versus long vowel contrast, e.g., -tim- 'become wet' and -tiim- 'graze cattle'. In a small number of cases, there may be no root-initial consonant. The initial consonant may be labialized, the final nasalized. Simple root types are given in Table 4.1.

Underlying -CV- roots, of which there are thirteen, are listed in Table 4.2. These produce three kinds of simple monosyllabic stems. Before a following vowel, underlying front vowels, /i/ or /e/, become [y], underlying /u/ becomes [w], while underlying /a/ is deleted.

Table 4.1 Simple root types

-CV-	-pa-	'give'			
-CVC-	-chek-	'slice'			
-CʷVC-	-mwetuk-	'flash'			
-CʸVC-	-syet-	'spit'			
-V:C-	-iit-	'name'	-V:ⁿC-	-iimb-	'perform'
-CV:C-	-baal-	'increase'	-CV:ⁿC-	-keend-	'chop'
-CʷV:C-	-pwaat-	'quarrel'	-CʷV:ⁿC-	-twiing-	'perspire'
-CʸV:C-	-pyeel-	'sweep'	-CʸV:ⁿC-	-myaand-	'lick'

Table 4.2 Monosyllabic stems

-C-a					
-ba	/-ba-/	'be(come)'	*-pa*	/-pa-/	'give'
-cha	/-či-/	'become day'	*-sha*	/-še-/	'grind'
-cha	/-či-/	'be sharp'			
-Cʸ-a			-Cʷ-a		
-lya	/-li-/	'eat'	*-fwa*	/-fu-/	'die'
-nya	/-ni-/	'defecate'	*-(g)wa*	/-(g)u-/	'fall'
-pya	/-pi-/	'become hot'	*-kwa*	/-ku-/	'pay brideprice'
-ya	/-i-/	'go'	*-lwa*	/-lu-/	'fight'
			-mwa	/-mu-/	'shave'
			-ng'wa	/-ŋu-/	'drink'
			-pwa	/-pu-/	'subside'
			-twa	/-tu-/	'sprout'

❖ **Complex radicals: Root expansion**

As in most Bantu languages, there are complex radicals in which one-time productive extensions have become lexicalized and are no longer perceived as separable elements. In these cases, the root never appears in the language without the extension, which is separated from the root in the following examples by a dot. Only those extensions that have become non-productive, or nearly so, are listed below. See the discussion of extensions for other examples.

• *-al-*

The Bantu EXTENSIVE element *-al-* is non-productive in Chindali. Although several words with this extension have a sense of being debilitated or ill in some way, there is no apparent overarching sense.

-ful.al-a	'be hurt'	*-aang.al-a*	'play'
-kal.al-a	'be angry'	*-bag.al-a*	'carry on shoulder'
-kaang.al-a	'be old'	*-bug.al-a*	'show development of motor skills'
-lem.al-a	'be lame'		
-yeyeb.al-a	'be weak'	*-iik.al-a*	'sit, live, stay'

63

- *-am-*

POSITIONAL-STATIVE element: This element indicated that the actor had assumed or was in a particular physical posture or position. It is essentially non-productive; only one verb exhibits a current derivational relationship.

-fif-am-a	'be hidden'	<	*-fifa*	'hide' *vt*

-fuk.am-a	'kneel'	*-iin.am-a*	'bend at waist'
-fuul.am-a	'bow'	*-kup.am-a*	'lie on belly'
-gal.am-a	'lie on back'	*-seend.am-a*	'become leaning'
-gas.am-a	'gape'	*-taand.am-a*	'back away from'
-iim.am-a	'be hidden'	*-aas.am-a*	'open the mouth'

- *-at-*

TENTIVE element: This general Bantu extension is non-productive in Chindali. A common thread in most words is a sense of 'clutch firmly'.

-finy'.at-a	'squeeze'	*-kam.at-a*	'wring'
-fuumb.at-a	'grasp in hand'	*-pak.at-a*	'hold in lap'
-fiik.at-a	'hold in arm'	*-pap.at-a*	'make a noise flapping off'

- *–Vp–*

STATIVE ATTRIBUTE: This extension is rare and, essentially, non-productive. Only one verb-to-verb derivation is known. The vowel is always that found in the original stem.

-soong-op-a	'be sharp, pointed'	<	*-soonga*	'sharpen to a point'
-oog.op-a	'be afraid'	(cf.	*ubw.ooga*	'fear')
-buul.up-a	'be faded'	<	*búu*	'very faded'
-eel.up-a	'be white'	<	*-eelu*	'white'
-swee.p-a	'be white'	<	*swée*	'snow-white'

- *Multiple elements*

Many words manifest two or more elements that have become lexicalized in the verb and no longer exhibit any morphological alternation with a simple root. Typically, the second element is the applicative extension *-il-*, which is highly productive in the language.

- *-am- + -il-*

-aat.am.il-a	'sit on [eggs]'
-eeg.am.il-a	'be leaning against'

- *-at- + -il-*

-fug.at.il-a	'take charge of'
-fuumb.at.il-a	'embrace'

- *-ik- + -il-*

-liimb.ik.il-a	'work hard'
-kop.ek.el-a	'become engaged'

- *-uk- + -il-*

-aamb.uk.il-a	'infect'
-ful.uk.il-a	'boil'
-seend.uk.il-a	'walk in an odd manner'

- *-ul- + -il-*

-lag.ul.il-a	'summon spirit'
-shuung.ul.il-a	'be round'

- *-il- + -ik-*

-pep.el.uk-a	'be blown by wind'

- *-ik- + -il- + -an-*

-tal.ik.il.an-a	'be far apart'

❖ Complex radicals: Reduplication

Radicals may also have derived from reduplication of some part of the root, or from reduplication of the stem. Only the reduplicated form is extant in modern Chindali. Partial reduplication consists of reduplication of the initial CV- sequence. Hence, original $-C_1V_1C_2-$ roots are now $-C_1V_1.C_1V_1C_2-$, while original -CV:C- roots have become either $-C_1V_1.C_1V_1:C_2-$ or $-C_1V_1:.$ $C_1V_1C_2-$. This type of reduplication appears to be non-productive in the modern language.

- Partial reduplication of the root:
  reduplicand–root [$-C_1V_1.C_1V_1C_2-$]

-ko.kot-a	'scrape food from pot'
-pu.put-a	'dry off'
-te.tem-a	'tremble' or 'overprotect'

65

- Partial reduplication of the root:
  reduplicand–root $[-C_1V_1.C_1V_1:C_2-]$

-ng'e.ng'ees-a	'gnaw'
-pa.paash-a	'grope'
-sa.saany-a	'convene'
-te.teesh-a	'move sth. carefully'

- Partial reduplication of the root:
  reduplicand–root $[-C_1V_1:.C_1V_1C_2-]$

-poo.posh-a	'make sth. dirty'
-see.sem-a	'move feet by shuffling'

❖ **Complex radicals: Reduplication plus expansion**

Some complex radicals have arisen from a combination of reduplication and addition of an extension.

-ye.yeb.al-a	'be pampered'	
-she.sh.een-a	'crush'	< -she + an- 'grind' + ??
-to.tom.el-a	'covet'	
-lu.luut.il-a	'ululate'	
-me.meek.el-a	'insist'	
-mwe.mweet.el-a	'smile'	
-ny'o.ny'oot.el-a	'squat'	
-na.nam.ish-a	'peek'	
-sa.sam.uk-a	'become cheerful'	
-to.tom.uk-a	'be surprised'	
-li.liimb.uk-a	'be sticky'	
-nya'.ny'aat.uk-a	'tiptoe'	
-ny'a.ny'aap.ul-a	'stick'	

❖ **Extensions and derivation**

Verbs may change valence by the addition of what are typically called verb extensions. There are twelve of these extensions that are at least somewhat productive in Chindali: *-an-/-aan-*[1] associative, *-an-/an-*[2] resultative, *-any-*

66

pluractional, *-ik-/-ek-₁* impositive, *-ul-/-ol-* separative active, *-ik-/-ek-₂* medio-passive, *-ik-/-ek-₃* causative, *-il-/-el-* applicative (or dative), *-ilil-/-elel-* persistive, *-ish-/-esh-₁* efferential, *-ish-/-esh-₂* intensive, and *-uk-/-ok-* separative medio-passive. The role and forms of each are provided below.

- *-an-₁ / -aan-₁*

ASSOCIATIVE: These related extensions denote some type of affiliation between two or more individuals, typically in the sense of RECIPROCITY, COLLECTIVITY, or COMITATIVITY. The same verb may permit different types of associative readings, depending on the singularity or plurality of the subject. The examples below illustrate just one possible reading of each verb.

Reciprocal

-koongana	'follow e. o.'	<	*-koonga*	'follow'
-lekana	'break up with e.o.'	<	*-leka*	'leave alone'
-pulikana	'agree with e. o.'	<	*-pulika*	'listen'
-shipana	'love e. o.'	<	*-shipa*	'propose intimacy'

Collective

-pimilana	'decide together'	<	*-pima*	'decide'
-pootana	'compete'	<	*-poota*	'defeat'

Miscellaneous with *-aan-*

-aafwaana (na)	'cooperate with'	<	*-aafwa*	'help'
-kolaana (na)	'resemble'	<	*-kola*	'touch'
-lekaana (na)	'part from'	<	*-leka*	'leave alone'
-oongaana	'mix together'	cf.	*-oongela*	'add to'

Lexicalized cases

-aambana	'quarrel'	*-buumbaana*	'be crowded tgthr'
-ny'aambana	'live far from e.o.'	*-buungaana*	'gather tgthr'
-paambana	'differ from e.o.'	*-komaana (na)*	'meet'
-taanana	'exchange'		

- *-an-₂ ~ -aan-₂*

RESULTATIVE: This extension reconfigures the event structure, removing both the agent causing the resulting state and the 'becoming' phase. The verb

-tukana 'swear' appears to be an idiosyncratic derivation using this extension. Compare this extension with *-ik-₂* on page 70.

-buluungana	'be round'	<	*-buluunga*	'make round'
-piindana	'be bent, twisted'	<	*-piinda*	'bend'
-saatana	'be scattered'	<	*-saata*	'scatter'
-palamana	'be near'	<	*-palamila*	'move near'
-tukana	'swear'	<	*-tuka*	'insult'

-aan- / -CVVNC-_____

-nyeengaana	'be coiled'	<	*-nyeenga*	'coil'
-nyoongaana	'be bent, twisted'	<	*-nyoonga*	'twist'
-tuungaana	'be knotted'	<	*-tuunga*	'knot'

-yuungaana	'be shaken; sway'
-luungaana	'be retarded'

• *-any-*

PLURACTIONAL: This extension indicates that an action is reiterated or that multiple subjects carry out the action.

Reiterated action

-chekanya	'cut into pieces' 'cut in many places'	<	*-cheka*	'slice'
-gabanya	'divide into parts'	<	*-gaba*	'divide'
-keendanya	'chop into pieces'	<	*-keenda*	'cut in two'
-ny'eepulanya	'tear into pieces'	<	*-ny'eepula*	'tear'
-putulanya	'break into pieces'	<	*-putula*	'break in two'
-saanganya	'chop into small pieces'	<	*-saanga*	'cut meat into pieces'

Multiple patients

-poondanya	'mash items together'	<	*-poonda*	'mash sth.'

Multiple subjects

-ny'amusanya	'carry together'	<	*-ny'amula*	'pick up & carry'

–ŋ–k–an–

A variant of the Pluractional extenison occurs with stems having stem-final [k]. In these cases, the stem-final [k] is prenasalized–[ŋk]–and followed by *-an-*.

-baluungana	'split in several places'	<	*-baluka*	'split' *vi*
-tuluungana	'burst in several places'	<	*-tuluka*	'burst' *vi*
-tapiingana	'vomit all over'	<	*-tapika*	'vomit'
-taliingana	'argue'	<	*-talika*	'argue'
-lamuungana	'greet one other'	<	*-lamuka*	'greet'
-kaangana	'quarrel'	<	*-kalala*	'be angry'

Two words occur with both types of marking:

-kupiinganya	'cover one plate with another'	<	*-kupika*	'turn top face down'
-patiinganya	'wear more than one item of clothing at once'			

- *-ik-1 ~ -ek-1* ⇔ *-ul- ~ -ol-*

IMPOSITIVE ⇔ SEPARATIVE (Active): These extensions are often commutable. They indicate physical placement of some object in or removal from some location, respectively.

-aanika	'put out to dry'	⇔	*-aanula*	'remove from drying'
-baatika	'put in order'	⇔	*-baatula*	'remove in order'
-fubika	'soak in water'	⇔	*-fubula*	'remove from water'
-fwiika	'put on clothes'	⇔	*-fuula*	'remove clothes'
-iifunika	'put a cover on'	⇔	*-iifunula*	'remove a cover'
-kupika	'cover'	⇔	*-kupukula*	'uncover'

In other cases, the impositive is simply added to the simple intransitive stem. The source verb may no longer be extant in the language in which case the extension has become lexicalized.

-baambika	'put in a line'	<	*-baamba*	'stand in line'
-kupamika	'lay s.o. face down'	<	*-kupama*	'lie face down'
-goneka	'lay s.o. down'	<	*-gona*	'lie down, sleep'

69

-matika	'stick sth. on'	<	-mata	'plaster on mud'
-fuundika	'put through a hole'			
-gaambika	'put a patch on'			
-iilika	'thatch'			
-iitwiika	'put on one's head'			

• -ik-2 ~ -ek-2

MEDIO-PASSIVE: The Medio-passive extension, like the Resultative described previously, reconfigures the event structure, rendering a transitive verb intransitive. Whereas the Resultatives denote the resultant effect of an activity, Medio-passives denote the state that is experienced.

-boneka	'be visible; look *vi*'	<	-bona	'see'
-malika	'be used up'	<	-mala	'finish'
-komanika	'be spoiled'	<	-komany'a	'spoil'
-piindika	'be bent'	<	-piinda	'bend'

It probably also occurs in the verb -pulikikwa 'be heard, be audible; sound', which has also affixed the passive extension -w-.

• -ik-3 ~ -ek-3

CAUSATIVE: This extension appears to be only marginally productive: only three verbs have been discovered derived with it. It changes event structure by adding a subject causer and demoting the agent from subject to object. Because it is so rare, an example of use is provided.

-imika	'make stand'	<	-ima	'stand'
-teenganika	'pacify'	<	-teengaana	'be comfortable'
-koleka	'make hold'	<	-kola	'hold'

ámafumu gakumukoleka   úmukolo umúfwiilwe ingwéego
6.chiefs   6.CC.1.hold.CAUS.F 1.woman 1.be_widowed 9.spear
'the chiefs make the widow hold a spear'

• -il- ~ -el-

APPLICATIVE: This extension, recently relabeled DATIVE (Schadeberg 2003), indicates that the action is carried out to an extreme (AUGMENTATIVE), on behalf of someone (BENEFACTIVE), in a manner directed away from the speaker (DIRECTIONAL), by means of or with a certain object (INSTRUMENTAL), at a certain place (LOCATIVE), or for a particular rea-son (PURPOSIVE). It may also be used simply to increase the valency of the verb.

70

The vowel alternates according to the quality of the preceding vowel: [e] following [e] or [o], [i] elsewhere.

Augmentative

-fikila	'settle'	<	*-fika*	'arrive'
-pulikila	'heed'	<	*-pulika*	'hear'
-shimila	'die out completely'	<	*-shima*	'die out'
-pakatila	'hold carefully'	<	*-pakata*	'hold'
-koolela	'shout loudly'	<	*-koola*	'shout'

Benefactive

-iilikila	'thatch for s.o.'	<	*-iilika*	'thatch'
-piiyila	'cook for s.o.'	<	*-piiya*	'cook'
-sukila	'wash sth. for s.o.'	<	*-suka*	'wash sth.'
-teshela	'look on behalf of'	<	*-tesha*	'look at'
-legela	'give way to'	<	*-lega*	'give way'

Directional

-buulila	'report sth. to s.o.'	<	*-buula*	'say, explain'
-iibunila	'hum to oneself'	<	*-buna*	'hum'
-kesela	'bark at'	<	*-kesa*	'bark'
-peela	'give to'	<	*-pa*	'give'
-syetela	'spit on'	<	*-syeta*	'spit'

Instrumental

-liila	'eat with'	<	*-lya*	'eat'
-suungila	'preserve with'	<	*-suunga*	'preserve'
-eengela	'brew using'	<	*-eenga*	'brew'
-komela	'beat with'	<	*-koma*	'beat'
-seengela	'build using'	<	*-seenga*	'build'

Locative

-gonela	'lie on sth.'	<	*-gona*	'lie down'
-ookolela	'transplant'	<	*-ookola*	'transfer'
-pululila	'go past a place'	<	*-pulula*	'go past'

71

Purposive

| *-lwiila* | 'fight over' | < | *-lwa* | 'fight' |
| *-piikila* | 'lie about s.o.' | < | *-piika* | 'tell a lie' |

Simple increase in valency

-hobokela	'forgive'	<	*-hoboka*	'be satisfied, pleased'
-soondela	'point out to s.o.'	<	*-soonda*	'point at sth.'
-taangila	'precede'	<	*-taanga*	'be first'

In many verbs it has become lexicalized, as in the examples below.

-tegela	'listen carefully'	[Augmentative]
-biyila	'move closer to'	[Directional]
-baandila	'catch fish with hands'	[Instrumental]
-fukila	'bury an object'	[Locative]
-tuungila	'come for a reason'	[Purposive]

• *-ilil- ~ -elel- (~ -eel-?)*

PERSISTIVE: The Persistive indicates that the action denoted by the verb exceeds what is expected with the usual action, either in duration (EXTENSIVE) or intensity (INTENSIVE). In some instances, the new lexical item has a slightly idiosyncratic meaning. The vowel alternates according to the preceding vowel: [e] following [e] or [o], [i] elsewhere. Stem final *-il-/-el-* loses the [l] when followed by *-ilil-*.

EXTENSIVE

-buukilila	'go beyond'	<	*-buuka*	'go'
-liindilila	'wait'	<	*-liinda*	'wait'
-keetelela	'watch'	<	*-keeta*	'look at'
-teshelela	'watch'	<	*-tesha*	'look at'
-pitiilila	'oversleep'	<	*-pitila*	'sleep soundly'
-goneelela	'sleep too long'	<	*-gonela*	'spend the night someplace'

INTENSIVE

| *-kiindilila* | 'rush' | < | *-kiinda* | 'run' |
| *-oogeela* | 'swim' | < | *-ooga* | 'bathe' *vi* |

72

• *-ish-*₁ ~ *-esh-*₁

EFFERENTIAL: This extension has traditionally been labeled a causative in Bantu studies. However, many verbs derived with it have the sense of action away from an actor, hence, an efferential function rather than a simple causative one (see Newman 1983 for discussion of efferential).

Action away from actor

-aambukisha	'infect' [by human]	⇔	*-aambukila*	'infect' [of diseas
-gulisha	'sell'	<	*-gula*	'buy'
-kopesha	'lend'	<	*-kopa*	'borrow'
-liisha	'feed'	<	*-lya*	'eat'
-many'isha	'teach, inform'	<	*-many'a*	'know'
-ny'alisha	'disgust'	<	*-ny'ala*	'become dirty'
-oongesha	'suckle'	<	*-oonga*	'suck'
-pulikisha	'listen to'	<	*-pulika*	'hear'
-wiisha	'drop sth.'	<	*-wa*	'fall'

Action away from patient

-kokotesha	'scrape away'	<	*-kokota*	'scrape'
-lipisha	'exact payment from'	<	*-lipa*	'pay sth.'

Simple transitivizing

-eendesha	'run' [of a machine]	<	*-eenda*	'go'
-fiitisha	'blacken'	<	*-fiita*	'become black'
-kalalisha	'anger'	<	*-kalala*	'be angry'
-lilisha	'make s.o. cry'	<	*-lila*	'cry'
-luumbisha	'face sth. toward'	<	*-luumba*	'turn toward'
-ponesha	'save s.o. from'	<	*-pona*	'escape injury'
-ny'aamisha	'engender'	<	*-ny'aama*	'increase in number'
-swiigisha	'surprise'	<	*-swiiga*	'be surprised'

Although the efferential function typically adds an argument to the verb, with an inherent three-argument verb such as *-laanga* 'show someone something' or *-iita* 'give a name to', it reduces the argument structure to two, placing focus on the secondary object.

-iitisha	'call to s.o.'	<	-iita	'give (a name) to'
-laangisha	'show to s.o.'	<	-laanga	'show s.o. sth'
-piikisha	'lie to s.o.'	<	-piika	'tell a lie'

- **-ish-2 ~ -esh-2**

INTENSIVE: This extension adds the sense of carrying out the action to a greater degree than that expressed by the simple stem. The vowel alternates according to the height of the preceding stem vowel.

-kaanisha	'prevent, prohibit'	<	-kaana	'deny'
-keetesha	'examine closely'	<	-keeta	'look at'
-laambilisha	'beg excessively'	<	-laamba	'beg'
-oongelesha	'add more to'	<	-oongela	'add'
-paalisha	'thank s.o.'	<	-paala	'compliment'
-suumilisha	'go about begging'	<	-suuma	'beg'
-gilimisha	'thunder'	<	-gilima	'roar'
-iikalisha	'sit properly'	<	-iikal	'sit'
-kokotesha	'scrape up every last scrap'	<	-kokota	'scrape'
-koongesha	'follow closely'	<	-koonga	'follow'
-loondesha	'seek'	<	-loonda	'look for'
-maliisha	'finish completely'	<	-mala	'finish'
-aandisha	'introduce'	<	-aanda	'start'
-siimbisha	'register'	<	-siimba	'write'
-pulikisha	'understand well'	<	-pulika	'understand'

- **-ul- ~ -ol- ⇔ -uk- ~ -ok-**

SEPARATIVE—Active vs Medio-passive: The two separative extensions indicate that some object has been separated from its neutral position or support. They differ in that the Active matches the semantic arguments agent and patient with the syntactic functions subject and patient, while the Medio-passive reduces the transitivity by removing the agent role and making the patient the syntactic subject.

-iigula	'open *vt*'	⇔	*-iiguka*	'open *vi*'
-kupula	'spill *vt*'	⇔	*-kupuka*	'spill out *vi*'
-ny'oongola	'break/cut off' *vt*	⇔	*-ny'oongoka*	'break off' *vi*
-pulula	'pick off'	⇔	*-puluka*	'drop off'
-satula	'tear seam thread' *vt*	⇔	*-satuka*	'tear [of seam]'
-suungunula	'melt' *vt*	⇔	*-suungunuka*	'melt' *vi*
-tupula	'blister' *vt*	⇔	*-tupuka*	'swell' *vi*
			[cf. *-tupa* 'be swollen']	

-iinula	'turn upright'	⇔	*-iinuka*	'be upright'
-kuumbula	'uproot'	⇔	*-kuumbuka*	'be uprooted'
-golola	'straighten'	⇔	*-goloka*	'be straight'
-ny'olola	'pierce'	⇔	*-ny'oloka*	'be pierced'
-pyoola	'break in two'	⇔	*-pyooka*	'be broken in two'

-aanula	'remove from drying'	⇔	*-aanika*	'put out to dry'
-baatula	'remove in order'	⇔	*-baatika*	'put in order'
-fubula	'remove from water'	⇔	*-fubika*	'soak in water'
-fuula	'remove clothes'	⇔	*-fwiika*	'put on clothes'
-iifunula	'remove a covering'	⇔	*-iifunika*	'put a covering on'
-kupukula	'uncover'	⇔	*-kupika*	'cover'

In a few instances, the separative alternates with a different extension.

-fukula	'disinter, dig up'	<	*-fukila*	'bury'
-fuumbula	'open hand'	<	*-fuumbata*	'close hand'

A few radicals, nearly all with the sense of removal, have lexicalized the separative.

-aatula	'remove sth. w/a needle'
-fyoogola	'remove ear from stalk'
-gelula	'remove a bit from'
-puupula	'wipe'
-satula	'unstitch'
-shuubula	'remove scab; skin'

Other cases with lexicalized *-ul-* have rather abstract senses of separation or simply lack any direct semantic connection to the typical sense.

-kobola	'pound with a pestle'
-fwogoombola	'make an opening in sth.'
-guchula	'eat undercooked yams'
-aagula	'yawn'

• Multiple extensions

In many cases, a verb may have multiple extensions. Lexicalization processes often obscure the sense, and even the form, of the extensions that have been attached.

Efferential + Associative

*-iit-is-**an**-y-a*	'call e. o.'	<	*-iitisha*	'call s.o.'
-yug-iis-an-y-a	'talk with e. o.'	<	*-yug-a*	'speak'

Impositive + Applicative.Causative

*-aan-ik-**ish**-a*	'dry by means of'	<	*-aanika*	'put out to dry'
-fum-ik-ish-a	'make come out by means of'	<	*-fuma*	'come out'

• Reduplication of the stem: [-CVC.a.CVC-a]

Reduplication of the verb stem may denote: (1) plural actors, (2) plural patients, (3) frequent reccurrence of the action, (4) iteration of the action, (5) intensity of action, (6) plurality of types.

• Plural actors

-seb.a.seb-a	'pick up' (pl)	<	*-seba*	'pick up'
-sek.a.sek-a	'laugh' (pl)	<	*-seka*	'laugh'

• Plural patients

-iimb.a.kw.iimb-a	'sing many songs'	<	*-iimba*	'sing'
-kuumb.a.kuumb-a	'dig up multiple items'	<	*-kuumba*	'dig'

• Frequency

-bin.a.bin-a	'get sick frequently'	<	*-bina*	'become ill'
-lw.a.ku.lw-a	'fight frequently'	<	*-lwa*	'fight'
-piik.a.piik-a	'lie often'	<	*-piika*	'lie'

• Iteration

-ny'eel.a.ny'eel-a	'jump repeatedly'	<	*-ny'eela*	'jump'
-eend.a.kw.eend-a	'roam about'	<	*-eenda*	'walk; go'
-sal.a.sal-a	'go around pecking at food'	<	*-sala*	'pick out'
-nyoongaan.a. nyoongaan-a	'be crooked in several places'	<	*-nyoongaana*	'be crooked'

• Intensive action

-cheb.a.cheb-a	'be very clever'	<	*-cheba*	'be clever'
-keet.a.keet-a	'look after'	<	*-keeta*	'look (at)'
-kol.a.kol-a	'feel'	<	*-kola*	'touch'
-loond.a.loond-a	'search for'	<	*-loonda*	'look for'

• Pluralized types

-kiindan.a.kiindan-a	'be of diff. kinds'	<	*-kiindana*	'be different'
-lekan.a.lekan-a	'be of diff. kinds'	<	*-lekana*	'differ'
-paamban.a. paamban-a	'be of diff. kinds'	<	*-paambana*	'differ from'
-yaan.a.yaan-a	'be similar, repetitive'	<	*-yaana*	'be of same type'

❖ Verb morphology: Constituent elements

As is typical of the Bantu languages, verb morphology in Chindali exhibits quite complex agglutination. As many as five grammatical categories may be expressed before and after the verb base; however, the number of categories expressed varies according to the mood (optional elements appear in plain text). Nevertheless, although not all moods express all categories, the nature and arrangement of the constituent categories is, generally, consistent with the template below. Note, however, that future proclitics are not described here, but rather in the discussion of non-indicative moods (see pages 132-135) and that the expression of negation differs from one mood to another.

SP– NEG– TMP– OM– **BASE** –ASP$_1$ –Vox –ASP$_2$ –**F** –ASP$_3$ =PoF

• Subject prefixes (SP)

The following subject prefixes are used for the respective human participants. See Table 3.1 for appropriate noun-class verb agreement prefixes. The variant *i-* in first-person singular occurs when the nasal form would be deleted for phonological reasons. Variants with the glide [w] occur before a vowel.

The second-person apodotic prefix is unusual. It typically is found (1) in the apodosis, or matrix clause, of a conditional sentence introduced by either *liinga* or *pala*, (2) in the apparently fossilized expressions with verb for 'find': *kwaaga* 'you find [that]', *kwaage* 'you may find [that]', *kwiisa kwaaga* 'you come to find [that]'.

		Singular		Plural
1		*n-, m-, i-*		*tu-, tw-*
2	Simple	*(g)u-, (g)w-*		*mu-, mw-*
	Apodotic		*ku-, kw-*	
3		*a-*		*ba-, b-*

tu-bóomb-e chóoni n'úbutolwe bwáá miishi ubú bwaatwaaga ichíinja íchi?
'what should we do about this problem of water that has come upon us this year?'

Apodotic *ku-*

bakuti pakabaangáápo íinguku shímo shíisho bakuti liingá w-áá-kola w-áá-ya w-aa-píiya kw-aagá naayímo múumwo w-aa-píiyite
'they say there used to be certain chickens which, they say, if you had caught [one] [and] had gone [and] cooked [it], you found it's not there where you cooked [it]'

78

*palá w-aa-púlika ipéenga **ku**-lekeesha imbóombo yóoshi*
'when you have heard the *ipenga* drum, you stop temporarily all work'

*liinga fishiku lyóo mukapimilaná lyaakwáana **ku**-mw-eega umúfuusha
yúla n-úugwe pamúpeéne mu-kw-aanda ubuléendo*
'when the day that you agreed to return arrives, you take the representative with you and, together, you [PL] begin the trip'

• Negative (NEG)

Negation is expressed in different positions according to the mood. In the Indicative mood, the negative marker *-ta-* occurs in this position.

• Tempus (TMP)

In the Tempus position occur markers relevant to the temporal reference of the event. There are three semantic sub-categories: Tense, Tenor, Event modality. Each of these is described in turn in Part 5.

Tense:	*-ka-*	[Remote]
Tenor:	*-ku-*	[Coincident]
	-aa-	[Anterior]
Event modality:	*-nga-*	[abilitive, permissive, general potentiality]

• Tense

Diverging from typical descriptions of tense, tense marking in this study denotes not the relationship between a point of reference, typically the time of the speech act, and the event named by the verb, but rather that between the cognitive world, or domain, in which the speech act is perceived to occur and a distinct, dissociated domain, which I label the P- and D-domains, respectively (see Botne 2003, 2006, and Botne & Kerschner 2008 for more detailed discussion and explanation of the model). In Chindali, the morpheme *-ka-* marks this relationship, often interpreted as denoting 'remoteness', past if the final vowel is *-a*, future if it is *-e*. In so-marking a verb, the speaker shifts the world of the narration to that D-domain. These relationships are schematized in Figure 4.1 (next page).

In this model, time is perceived in either of two ways: (1) Ego-moving along a temporal path from one domain to another, represented by line L from Past to Future, or (2) moving-Event, in which the event E is perceived as moving toward a fixed Ego (positioned at S) within the domain. This does not imply that there are two timelines; rather, there are two complementary views of time and the speaker's perceived relationship between self and event.

Figure 4.1. -*ka*- tense marking

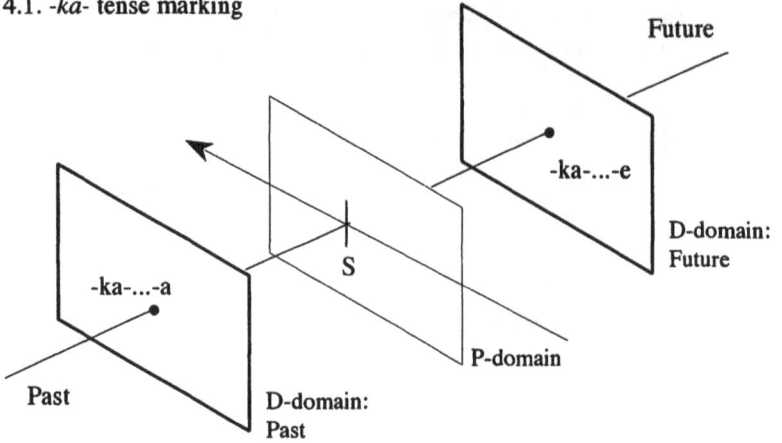

• **Tenor**

Tense, as stated above, refers to the relationship between events and the time of the speech event (S) across domains. However, temporal relationships can also be expressed within domains. The term adopted for this is TENOR. In Chindali, there are two morphemes that express tenor within a domain, -*ku*- and -*aa*-, labeled Coincident (CO) and Anterior (ANT), respectively. Coincident verb forms are interpreted as ongoing at the reference point, habitual, or generic. Without other context, simple tenor forms are interpreted within the P-domain, hence, anterior or non-anterior within that domain. The absence of either -*ku*- or -*aa*- is also relevant; hence, Ø tenor marking denotes a state.

• -*aa*-

Taking the P-domain for illustration, an Anterior (marked by -*aa*-) refers an event to the immediately preceding time period. That time period may be the time immediately preceding the speech event (S), yesterday if the relevant time unit is today, last year if the relevant time unit is this year, and so forth (schematically represented in Fig. 4.2). Final -*a* indicates that reference is to S

Figure 4.2. Anterior -*aa*-: anterior time units (AnTU) and the deictic center

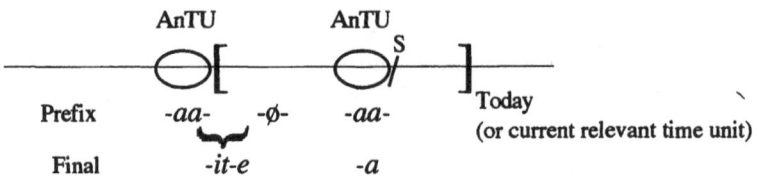

80

(the speech event), while -it-e indicates completion (see discussion under Aspect₁) of the nuclear phase of the event before then.

• *-ku-*

In contrast to *-aa-*, the morpheme *-ku-* denotes an event in some way coincident with the designated reference point, which may be the speech event (S) or some other event extablished in context. The event named by the verb may be (a) ongoing and current (hence, interpreted as progressive), (b) habitual (an activity that holds throughout the domain), or (c) generic (denotation that is considered to hold at any time). Illustrations in Figure 4.3 are for the P-domain, but would hold in a similar manner for a D-domain.

Figure 4.3. Possible representations of uses of *-ku-*

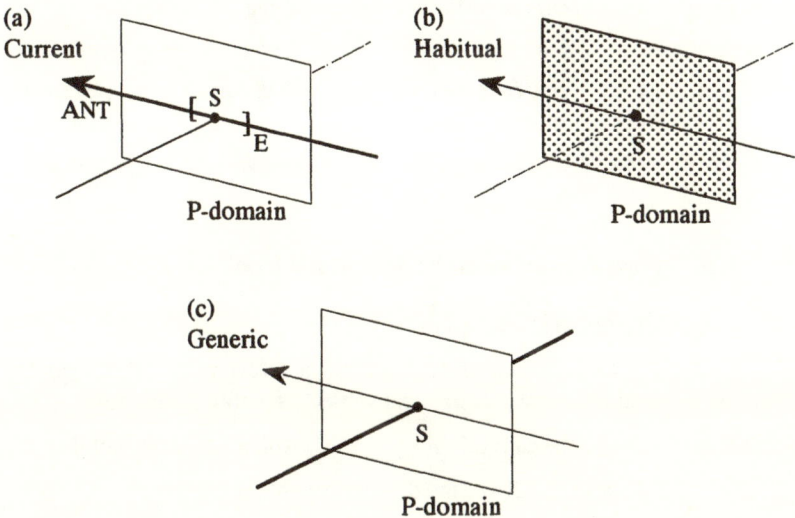

(a) Current — P-domain

(b) Habitual — P-domain

(c) Generic — P-domain

• **Event modality**

Whereas the Tense and Tenor categories denote the speaker's perception of the event with respect to the reference point, Event modality, following Palmer (2001), refers to the attitude of the speaker with respect to a potential future realization of the event. As such, it may express three kinds of modal perspective: abilitive, permissive, general potentiality. The marker is *nga-*.

• **Object marker** (OM) **and reflexive**

The OM position may have either an object marker agreeing with its noun, or the reflexive marker *-ii-*. Object markers for humans are presented below. See Table 3.1 for the appropriate forms of object markers for the various noun classes.

Person	1	2	3
Singular	*ny'-, n-, m-*	*ku-, kw-*	*mu-, mw-*
Plural	*tu-, tw-*	*ba-, b-*	*ba-, b-*

naapaalíshá ngááni kwáá tááta yúuyo aa-ny'-ááfwa léka
'I am very grateful to my father who is the one who has helped me a lot'

• *-ii-*

REFLEXIVE

A reflexive reading is given to the verbal unit by addition of the prefix *-ii-* (*-iiy-* before vowel-initial roots).

-ii-bega	'cut oneself'	<	*-bega*	'cut'
-ii-bunila	'hum to oneself'	<	*-buna*	'hum'
-ii-katisanya	'pile & carry load on one's head'	<	*-katisanya*	'pile & carry load on head'
-ii-teendekesha	'prepare oneself'	<	*-teendekesha*	'prepare'
-iiy-iima	'deny oneself sth.'	<	*-iima*	'abstain'

ak-iiy-ima íchaakúlya 'he denied himself food'

INTRANSITIVIZING FUNCTION

-ii- also has an intransitivizing function in a few verbs whereby it promotes an affected object to grammatical subject of a now stative verb:

-ii-kola	'be caught'	<	*-kola*	'hold'

iláaya l-ií-kola kuchikókwe 'the dress is caught on the bush'

-ii-gana	'want, desire; like'	<	*-gana*	'like, love'

n-ii-gan-ité ngááni ukuti imány'age fíifyo fikuboombiwa mufyíisu ífiingi
'I really want to know what happens in other countries'

wéeshi akufwaalá móo ii-gan-ífle 'each dresses the way s/he likes'

palá w-ii-ganíte 'if you like'

abáandu ábiingi ba-ta-ka-yi-gan-a isukúulu
'many people did not like school'

[Note: *n-ga-gan-íte ámatone* 'I like bananas']

• **Extensions** (Ext)

New forms of verbs may be derived through suffixation of one or more extensions. See previous description of extensions.

• **Aspect**

There are three verb "slots" relevant to aspectual marking of the verb, each offering a different aspectual perspective: Completive or Imperfective, the latter sub-divided into Collective and Individuated.

• **Asp$_1$**: Completive *-it..-e*

The first aspect slot is the Completive. The completive aspect is marked by the discontinuous morpheme *-it..-e*. Contextual variants occur:

-ile with monosyllabic stems, most bases ending with *l*, and *-iisa* 'come';

-iche with bases ending in *ch* [č];

-iishe with bases ending in *sh* [ʃ] , *y*, or *ny'* [ɲ].

-ng'wa	>	*-ng'wiile*
-bugala	>	*-bugiile*
-iisa	>	*-iisile*
-oocha	>	*-oochiiche*
-iingisha	>	*-iingishiishe*
-oobeesha	>	*-oobeeshiishe*
-tamya	>	*-tamyiishe*
-koosha	>	*-kooshiishe*
-iituufya	>	*-iituufyiishe*
-komany'a	>	*-komany'iishe*

With *l*-final bases, the morpheme is imbricated, hence, -CVCV-i(t)-l-e > -CVCG-ii-l-e. Two verbs, *-bona* 'see' and *-many'a* 'know', have idiosyncratic imbricated forms: *-bweeni* and *-meeny'e*, respectively.

The completive indicates that the nuclear, or characteristic, phase of the event has been completed. That is, the aspectual perspective is from a point (♦) following the nucleus (N). With Activity and Accomplish verbs, such as *-lima* 'cultivate, hoe' and *-bweela* 'return home', respectively, whose nuclei constitute the whole of the duration of the event, the perspective is outside of the event and is, consequently, interpreted as anterior to the point at which the (♦) is indexed. For Achievement verbs, on the other hand, whose nucleus is a

83

point followed by a durative coda phase, the event is interpreted as being in a state at that point. These perspectives are schematized below.

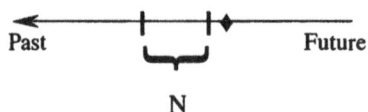

Activity or Accomplishment

tu-chi-l-ííl-e 'we ate it'

a-kam-ít-e 's/he milked'

Resultative Achievement

tu-méény'e 'we know'

a-lit-ít-e 's/he is tired'

Completive aspect marking co-occurs only with the Tenor prefixes, not with the Tense or Event modality prefixes of the Tempus position.

• **Asp₂ and Asp₃**: Imperfectives

-ag- (Collective) and *-aa* (Individuated)

The Aspect₂ and Aspect₃ slots contain imperfective suffixes, differentiated by whether they denote a collective or an individuated view of the event. Contextual variants of *-ag-* occur:

-aang- (i) when following a glide (in monosyllabic bases (-CG-), or

(ii) when following one of the subject valency-changing extensions, *-y-* Causative or *-w-* Passive, or

(iii) when following stems ending on the surface with *sh* [ʃ] (generally from underlying C + *y*);

-iingi when attached to the defective verb *-ti* 'say'.

Imperfective *-ag-* occurs in all moods, *-aa* only in the Indicative and Presumptive.

Imperfective *-ag-* expresses an external, collective view of the whole event in contrast to *-aa*, which expresses an internal, individuated view of the event [cf. Kershner 2001 and 2002:§5.2 for a detailed discussion of the imperfective in closely related Chisukwa]. Both may express the duration of the event over a long period in the remote past, typically translated as 'used to'. However, *-ag-* stresses the collective view of the whole event, *-aa* the individuation within.

• Past habitual vs distributive events

Collective: *ba-k-iimb-**ag**-a pakabalílo kaa pábushiku soóna*
              *ba-ka-cheelesh-**áang**-a*
              'they used to perform at night and also
              they used to do so all night long'

Individuated: *aboosékulu ba-ka-say-**aa** íifula kumashéeto*
'our grandparents used to make sacrifices for rain
at the "masheto" hut'

Collective: *pábulime bwáabo ba-ka-boombel-**ag**-a ímbiindulila*
'in their cultivating, they used to use irrigation ditches'

Individuated: *namáanga ábééne ba-ka-boombel-**aa** amákweéla*
ngáti poo yáába ngúbo
'you know, they, themselves, used to use animal skins
as though they were cloth'

Collective: *aboosékulu ba-ka-ba-buush-**aang**-a abóótááta ukuti*
liinga úbubine bukutamya pákaaya, bwoo bashúúka
bakalalíte
'our grandfathers used to tell our fathers, "if sickness
is plaguing the family, it means the spirits of the dead
are angry"'

Individuated: *abany'afyáale ba-ka-ba-buush-**aa** abáandu ukuti*
*mu-bóomb-**aa** ífyaakúti, fímo many'é mu-bóómb-**aa**,*
mwíiko.
'chiefs used to tell people,"you [PL] should do such-
and-such things, some things you [PL] should not do,
it's prohibited'

Collective: *úkúúbi akayibuula íinguku akati liingá utákuyaaga*
*isindáano yáangu, tí-n-gól-**ag**-e sóóna tí-n-dy-**áang**-e*
ábaana báako
'Chickenhawk told Chicken, it said, "if you do not find
my needle, I will catch and eat your chicks" '

Individuated: *weyúuyo akweenda akutuywaasha pánu á-ti a-ku-y-**aa***
pakúlima kulúundo úko
'he is the one who passes by and talks to us here when-
(ever) he goes to farm nearby there'

The following two examples illustrate cases in which a collective and an
individuated perspective alternate in the same sentence.

Collective	Individuated
*ba-k-iimb-**ag**-á mupáka abóóbiisa báande ukúúbika,*	*poo ba-k-aand-**aa** ukulekáana*
'they used to perform until roosters began crowing,	then they began to disperse'

Individuated	Collective
*ba-ka-pok-**áá** búu ífyaakúlya paamáka;* 'they just took food by force, according to the strength [of each];	*ba-k-iib-**ag**-a pábushiko* they used to steal at night'

In the following samples, an initially individuated perspective shifts to a collective perspective of a subsequent event.

Individuated	Collective
*bóoshi pákaaya ba-k-iitisany-**áa**,* 'everyone in the family called one another;	*ba-sáy-**ag**-e ukuti abashúúka* *ba-hóbok-e* they would [give a] sacrifice so that the spirits would be happy'
*ba-ka-baamb-**aa** ábakolo béene,* *abáliisha béene,* 'they stood in line, women only, men only,	*poo ba-komáán-**ag**-e* *pakáti* then they would meet in the middle'
*ba-ka-y-**aa** pakwiipuuta mukayúumba* *kála kála* 'they used to go to pray in that hut	*ukuti íifula yi-w-**áang**-e* *ákiisa* so that it would rain well'

*ichiméle ba-k-iimb-**ag**-á bóoshi abáliisha n'ábakolo pamúpeéne.*
'chimele they performed both men and women together'

*ábaana n'aboowíise ba-ka-gon-**aa** pamúpééne mpáka íse báfike*
pakabalílo káá bweegi
'children and parents used to sleep together [i.e., share the same house] until they reached the time for marriage'

• Continuous use

Collective event perspective

palá waapúlika ipéenga kulekeesha imbóombo yóoshi yóo
*w-aa-bóómb-**ag**-a n'ukukiindilila ukubuuka kubúyo bwaa*
mbúungo
'when you hear the ipenga drum, you stop temporarily all work
that you are doing and rush to go to the site of the funeral'

*n-(aa-)iinong'ón-**ag**-a ukuti chiyúni chíkulú ngááni*
chóócho chikukúuta
'I was thinking that it was a very big bird that was making
the loud noise'

*a-t-aa-yúg-**ag**-a ukuti twíímame náshiku*
'he was not saying that we should hide, not at all'

Individuated perspective

n-gu-liindilil-aa úNdeembwa 'I'm waiting for Ndembwa'

tí-n-júg-aa ichi pálwááke ichi pálwááke
'I will be talking about each [topic] separately'

ísa abaapáángila mwóo fikabéela namwóo a-ka-binil-a-biníl-aa
'it came about [that] he explained to them how things were and
how he was frequently sick'

• Generic

Collective

íinjoká yííyo báti yi-kw-áák-ag-a pábushiku
'that snake, they say, glows/shines at night'

liingá twíígana tu-ku-mog-ag-a páchaaka na pachilísimaasi
'if we like, we dance on New Year's Day and at Christmas'

Individuated

ímuumba yíiyo yaapaapíwa yi-ku-b-áá yaa múliisha, soóna
úmukolo weyúuyo a-ku-y-aa kúkaaya kaa múliisha
'the family who are born belong to the man, and the woman is
the one who goes to the home of the man'

abany'afyáale bakabá báandu abasálíwa bóó ba-ka-loongosh-aa ichíisu
'chiefs were chosen people who led the land'

soóna ba-tá-ka-boombel-aa ámakasu, i'í, lóole ifikókwe
n'amábwe ámakole
'also, they did not use hoes, no, but [rather] sticks and sharp rocks'

báti poo íinguku shi-ku-palasany-aa mwilóóngwi, báti
shi-ku-loond-áá sindáano yáá kuúbi.
'they say, then, chickens scratch in the soil, looking, they say,
for chicken hawk's needle'

Finally, here are two examples that appear to reference the collective
actors or the indviduated positions associated with the events.

mufiny'ámáana fyóoshi fyóo fi-ka-kuumb-ag-a akashíme,
mutákabáámo naayúmo umugáanga yóo akamany'a ukutiisha
utúundu twóo twááya múmaaso
'among all the animals that dug the well, there was among them
not one medicineman who knew how to remove little things from
the eyes'

ilambílaambi ílyo li-ka-shigil-áá báti pándaashi na paany'úma
péene mbáasi
'that bark cloth covered, they say, in the front and in the back only'

87

• Voice-changing extensions (Vox)

Two extensions occur in this position, Causative *-y-* and Passive *-iw-*. Like other extensions, these function to change the valency of the verb. They differ from other extensions in two significant ways: (1) they attract the verbal high tone, removing it from ante-penultimate position, and (2) they reconfigure the linking of grammatical and thematic roles. Passive *-iw-* promotes a patient or goal from object to subject role, while Causative *-y-* demotes an agent from subject to object role, while concomitantly adding a Causer argument as subject of the verb.

• PASSIVE: *-iw-* ~ *-ibw-* ~ *-ikw-* ~ *-igw-* ~ *-w-*

The passive typically requires that the recipient or goal of the action denoted by the verb be the grammatical subject. The most common form is *-iw-*; the others occur sporadically.

-eegiwa	'be married'	<	*-eega*	'marry'
-loondiwa	'be needed'	<	*-loonda*	'need, want'
-lumiwa	'be bitten by'	<	*-luma*	'bite'
-paapiwa	'be born by'	<	*-paapa*	'give birth to'
-sayiwa	'be blessed by'	<	*-saya*	'bless'
-kopwa	'be owed by'	<	*-kopa*	'borrow'
-gunwa	'be cursed by'	<	*-guna*	'put a spell on'
-tamiwa	'be afflicted by'	<	*-tamya*	'be difficult; be a problem'
-kuumbibwa	'be dug'	<	*-kuumba*	'dig'
-saamilibwa	'be transplanted'	<	*-saamila*	'move to a place'
-tipibwa	'be dug deep'	<	*-tipa*	'dig deep'
-many'ikwa	'be known'	<	*-many'a*	'know'
-pulikikwa	'be heard'	<	*-pulika*	'hear'
-paangigwa	'be made'	<	*-paanga*	'make'

88

• CAUSATIVE: -y-

The -y- causative is a highly productive extension. It reconfigures the event structure by adding a new argument, the causer, to the semantic structure of the verb, hence, intransitive verbs become transitive, transitive become ditransitive.

This extension effects changes in the preceding consonant of the stem. Nasals become palatalized [m, n > mʸ, nʸ]; labials become spirantized [b, p > fʸ]; others become *sh* [t, d, l, k, g > ʃ]. Examples below illustrate its form with different sets of verbs.

• m, n > mʸ, nʸ

-fuulamya	'make s.o. bend'	<	*-fuulama*	'bend' *vi*
-shimya	'extinguish'	<	*-shima*	'go out (of a fire)'
-binya	'make s.o. sick'	<	*-bina*	'be sick'

• b, p > fʸ

-kifya	'make s.o. endure pain'	<	*-kiba*	'endure pain'
-sofya	'lose sth.'	<	*-soba*	'be lost'
-oogofya	'frighten'	<	*-oogopa*	'be afraid'

• t, d, l > ʃ

-fuusha	'make s.o. breathe'	<	*-fuuta*	'breathe'
-kiisha	'chase sth. away'	<	*-kiinda*	'run'
-myaasha	'make s.o. lick'	<	*'myaanda*	'lick'
-eegamisha	'put in a leaning position'	<	*-eegamila*	'be leaning against sth.'
-iisusha	'fill'	<	*-iisula*	'be full'
-fulukisha	'boil sth.'	<	*-fulukila*	'boil' *vi*
-fulasha	'hurt s.o.'	<	*-fulala*	'be hurt'
-fwaasha	'put [clothes] on s.o.'	<	*-fwaala*	'put [clothes] on oneself'
-iikasha	'seat s.o.'	<	*-iikala*	'sit'
-iingisha	'usher s.o. in'	<	*-iingila*	'enter'
-iigusha	'make s.o. open'	<	*-iigula*	'open' *vt*

• k, g > ʃ

-eengusha	'melt' *vt*	<	*-eenguka*	'melt' *vi*
-golosha	'make straight'	<	*-goloka*	'be straight'
-hobosha	'please s.o.'	<	*-hoboka*	'be pleased, happy'
-sefusha	'boil' *vt*	<	*-sefuka*	'boil up' *vi*
-galusha	'bring back sth.'	<	*-galuka*	'go back'
-ny'oosha	'return sth.'	<	*-ny'ooka*	'remain behind'
-oosha	'wash s.o.'	<	*-ooga*	'wash oneself'
-nuusha	'smell' *vt*	<	*-nuunga*	'smell' *vi*

In some instances, the derived meaning is idiosyncratic, as in the following examples.

-chefya	'outwit, deceive'	<	*-cheba*	'be clever'
-binya	'care for' [med.]	<	*-bina*	'be sick'
-kusha	'raise a child'	<	*-kula*	'grow up'
-hobosha	'be interesting'	<	*-hoboka*	'be happy, pleased'
-tamya	'be difficult'	<	*-tama*	'be overwrought'

• **Final** (F)

There are two stem-final vowels, *-a* and *-e*. The first, *-a*, can be considered the neutral element, used whenever *-e* is not. Final *-e* appears in the following contexts:

(i) as part of the completive aspect, *-it*...-e;

(ii) in imperative constructions having a prefixed object marker (OM);

(iii) non-indicative moods (except simple bare imperative).

• **Post-final enclitics** (PoF)

The post-final elements express locative, theme, partitive, and adverbial functions.

• Locative elements

-po

> *wée fyóoshi we fikabáápo palukomáano*
> 'all of them [animals] were **there** at this meeting'

90

táangiiséépo soóna pánu 'I will never again come *here*'

pámwaany'a pákasale bakupikitéépo íifugo
'on top of the roof they placed *there* a bugali cooking pot'

-ko ~ -kwo

ichipéépala chóo cháali kúchaaka chaany'any'áápuka chatíilááko
'the plastic that was on the handle has become stretched and come off'

akati isóopo shitákabááko n'ámafuta
'he said there was no soap and oil [=lotion]'

pepeekááko ichíigi 'close the door a bit'

akasaamááko kwáá Njebete 'he moved away from Njebete'

lóole ábééne fikabá fyíisáápo páapo báti abalóshi batákabáákwo
'but for them things were better because they say there were no witches then'

akamusuuma uSílúúmbu ukuti ábape ubúyo bwaakuti biikalagéékwo
'he asked that Silumbu give them a place to live there'

tutíiléékwo kubúyo búla 'we should leave that place'

-mwo

akabalekela iny'úúmba yaa kupiiyáámwo ukuti biikalagéémwo
'he left them a cooking house so that they could live there'

ímishitu yilíímwo mítatu 'the forests are three'

ugáany'u wáake akabaangá waa kukuumbula íindete ukwiiguláá-mwo umugúunda
'his piecework was digging out reeds to open a field'

- Theme

-po 'about'

bakiinong'ona ukuti babóombéépo shímo
'they decided that they would do something *about* it'

akuloonda pakuyugáápo fímo
'he wants to speak *about* something'

- Partitive

-po 'a bit'

abenembúungo bakuyugáápo ukupaalisha páfyaa bútuuli
'relatives of the deceased speak *briefly* thanking [people] for the help'

ichiny'ámáana chóoshi chikakolagáápo imbóombo
'each animal took on *some* work'

likubáápo íishiku líilyo bóoshi bakukomáana
'there is a day when all meet'

• Adverbial

-nga 'only then; now that this has happened'

> *palá aalípila poo akwaandáanga pakushíingila*
> 'when he has paid, *only then* does he begin to propose marriage'

> *tíbabonéenga* '*only then* will they see'

> *palá náámala imbóombo shóoshi poo tímbuúkagéenga pakuyáata*
> 'when I finish all the chores, *only then* I will go for a stroll'

> *akiituufya ukuti poo bachebiteenga?*
> 'he was boasting, saying "so, are they clever, *now that this has happened*?"'

-she 'just'

> *aáma akiikaláashe* 'well, she was *just* living there'

> *akusuumbáashe* 'she *just* keeps quiet'

> *abáandu bábili ába baayáánitééshe úbutali*
> 'these two people were *just* of the same height'

-po 'as well'

> *usékulu akapaapáápo n'ábaana ábakolo bábili báabo boo-*
> *náséénge báangu*
> 'grandfather even fathered *as well* two daughters who are
> my aunts'

• Sequencing of PoF elements

The post-final elements can co-occur in some cases. The examples below show that the locative and partitive enclitics precede the adverbial enclitcs. The adverbial enclitics are also ordered, with *-she* 'just' preceding *-nga* 'only then'.

Locative before Adverbial enclitic

> *pyeeláá-poó-she* '*just* sweep *there*' [i.e., no need to mop]

Partitive before Adverbial enclitic

> *lim-áá-poó-she* '*just* cultivate *a little*'

> *lim-ag-áá-poó-she* 'keep cultivating *just a little* (longer)'

Adverbial *-she* before adverbial *-nga*

palá náámala imbóombo shóoshi poo tímbuúk-ag-eé-shee-nga
'when I finish all the chores, *only then* I will *just* be going'
[as in 'I'll just do this' since there is nothing else to do]

PART 5

VERB TYPES

Verbs differ in the kind of internal phase structure they have. Differences in these structures affect the way in which they interact with tense, tenor, and aspect marking. The categorization that follows is a preliminary assessment, illustrating the different types, the nature of their internal structure, and evidence that supports the classification. Among diagnostic constructions are the following: imperatives, coincident (CO) -ku- constructions, -li pa-INF, completive -Ø...ite, and occurrence or meaning with aspectualizing verbs such as -leka 'cease' or -mala 'finish'. There appear to be four major categories of verbs identified by these tests: Activity verbs, Accomplishment verbs, Achievement verbs, and Stative verbs. Accomplishment and Achievement verbs can be further sub-categorized.

❖ **Activity verbs**

Activity verbs constitute a large class of verbs that are characterized by a durative nuclear activity phase during which the event can be said to be on-going. There is no inherent endpoint encoded in the verb itself. Such verbs have the following properties:

- they occur in the imperative;
- they occur in the -li pa-INF construction;
- they occur with -ku-, having the sense 'in the midst of V-ing'
- they co-occur with the aspectual auxiliaries -leka 'cease; stop' or -mala 'finish'

Some verbs of this type:

-iimba	'perform'	-lya	'eat'
-kama	'milk'	-moga	'dance'
-lima	'cultivate, hoe'	-puuta	'blow [e.g., on a fire]'

Examples of use:

mogága	'dance'
a-li pa-kú-moga	's/he is dancing'
a-kú-mog-a	's/he is [in the midst of] dancing'
a-mog-íte	's/he danced' [earlier today]
áá-mog-a	's/he has [just] danced'
aa-móg-ite m'masuba	's/he danced yesterday'
kama ulúkama	'milk the milk'
a-ku-kam-a ulúkama	's/he is [in the midst of] milking'
a-kaa-lí a-kú-kama	's/he is still milking'
a-kam-íte	's/he milked earlier' [today]
áa-li pa-kúkama	's/he was milking' [today]
aa-kám-ite	's/he milked' [yesterday]
a-ka-ba pa-kúkama	's/he was milking' [yesterday]

97

❖ **Accomplishment verbs**

Accomplishment verbs are very similar to Activity verbs in that they both encode durative nuclear phases. They differ in that Accomplishment verbs have an inherent endpoint, a coda. The coda may be either a point or a phase.

• Simple Accomplishment verbs

These verbs have the following properties:

• they occur in the imperative;
• they occur in the -li pa-ku-INF construction;
• they occur with -ku- with a progressive meaning;
• they do not co-occur with the aspectual auxiliary -mala 'finish'.

They have the following temporal phase structure:

```
 _____
|           |
 ‾‾‾‾‾‾‾‾‾‾‾
  N    C
```

Some verbs of this type:

-aanda	'begin'
-poota	'defeat'

mupoóte	'defeat him'
ba-ku-mu-póot-a	'they're defeating him'
ba-mu-poot-íte	'they defeated him' [earlier today]
ba-kaa-lí ba-ku-mu-póot-a	's/he is still returning home'
b-aa-mu-póot-a	'they have just defeated him'

• Transitional Accomplishment verbs

Transitional Accomplishment verbs differ from Simple Accomplishments in that they encode a durative coda phase (rather than simply a coda final point). This coda phase represents a state attained by virtue of car-rying out the characteristic (or nuclear) activity of the verb. Such verbs have the following properties:

• they occur in the -li pa-ku-INF construction;
• they occur with -ku- with a progressive meaning;
• they occur in the perstitive construction, SP-kaali SP-ku-RAD-a, meaning 'still carrying on activity';
• they occur in the current completive, indicating a state;
• they don't occur with -mala 'finish'.

They have the following temporal phase structure:

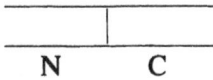

```
 _____|_____
    N         C
```

Some verbs of this type:

-fwaala	'dress'
-fuula	'undress'

fwaála	'dress'
a-ku-fwáal-a	's/he's dressing' [now]
a-fuul-íte	's/he is undressed'
	's/he undressed' [earlier today]
a-kaa-lí a-ku-fúul-a	's/he is still undressing'
a-kaa-lí a-fuul-íte	's/he is still undressed'

❖ Achievement verbs

Achievement verbs differ from Activities and Accomplishments in that they have a punctual, rather than a durative, nuclear phase. They are of four types—Acute, Inceptive, Resultative, and Transitional—depending on whether or not they also encode an onset and/or coda phase. An onset phase is a coming to be, the coda a state of being.

• Acute

Acute achievement verbs encode the named event as a point with no perceived temporal duration, no onset phase, and no coda phase. Such verbs have the following properties:

- they do not occur in the imperative;
- they do not occur in the *-li pa-INF* construction;
- they have the sense of 'about to' or 'current state' with *-ku-*;
- they have the sense of 'current state' with *-aa-*;
- they do not occur in the perstitive construction SP-kaa-li SP-ku-RAD-a;
- they do not occur with either auxiliary *-leka* 'cease' or *-mala* 'finish'.

They have the following temporal phase structure:

```
  |
  N
```

Some verbs in this class are the following:

-cheetwa 'be late'

-fika 'arrive'

a-ku-chéétw-a	's/he's (always) late'
n-aa-chéétw-a kumbóombo	'I'm late for work'
a-cheet-ít-w-e	's/he is late' [now]

a-kú-fik-a 's/he's about to arrive' [e.g., approaching the door]

mwoo ba-kú-fik-a, bakabááshe banáandi
'when they arrived, there were just a few of them'

ábakamu ábiingi ábaa múbutali likubá líshiku lyaakuti
   b-áá-fik-a pakúlila
'for relatives from far away, it is the day on which
   they arrive to mourn'

tukwaanda pakumany'ila iny'áando ukuti liinga ichipaláano
   ch-áá-fik-a tukámogage ákiisa
'we begin to learn the basics so that when the competition
  arrives, we will dance well'

• Inceptive

Inceptive achievement verbs encode an onset phase in addition to the punctual nulear phase. Such verbs have the following properties:

- they do not occur in the imperative;
- they do not occur in the *-li pa-INF* construction;
- they have a future reading with *-ku-*;
- they have a present stative reading in the construction *-Ø...-ite*.

They have the following temporal phase structure:

O N

Some verbs of this type:

-pola 'heal'

chi-ku-pol-a	'it [e.g., wound] is healing'
chi-pol-íte	'it is healed'
ch-áá-pol-a	'it has healed'
chi-kaa-lí chi-kú-pol-a	'it's still healing'

• Resultative

Resultative achievement verbs encode a coda phase in addition to the punctual nulear phase, but do not encode an onset phase. Such verbs have the following properties:

- • they do not occur in the imperative;
- • they do not occur in the *-li pa-INF* construction;
- • they have only a habitual or generic reading with *-ku-*;
- • they do not occur with in the perstitive construction;
- • they have a present stative reading in the construction *-Ø...-ite*.

They have the following temporal phase structure:

```
 ┌──────┐
 │
 N    C
```

Some verbs of this type:

-hoboka	'be happy'	*-lita*	'be tired'
-lemala	'be lame'	*-moga*	'be pretty'

Examples of use:

a-lemiíle	's/he's lame'
a-kú-lita	's/he is usually tired'; 's/he tires'
a-ku-lit-á n'imbóombo	's/he tires with work'
a-lit-ít-e	's/he is tired'
aa-lít-it-e	's/he was tired'
áá-lit-a	's/he has tired'
á-hobok-ite	's/he's happy' [now and in general]
tw-aa-hóbok-a	'we have beome happy' [now]

• Transitional

Transitional achievement verbs encode both an onset and a coda phase in addition to the punctual nulear phase. This class, along with Activity verbs, constitute the largest verb classes in Chindali. Such verbs have the following properties:

- • they do not occur in the imperative;
- • they do not occur in the *-li pa-INF* construction;
- • they have either a coming-to-be or a habitual or generic reading with *-ku-*;
- • negation of Coincident *-ku-* negates the onset phase;
- • they have a present stative reading in the construction *-Ø...-ite*;
- • they do not occur in the perstitive construction with *-ite* on the main verb and have a current stative reading.

101

Transitional achievement verbs have the following temporal phase structure:

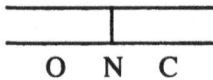

Some verbs of this type:

-pola	'become cold'	*-bala*	'be(come) bright/shiny'
-pya	'become hot'	*-iikala*	'sit'
-tona	'become ripe'	*-fwa*	'die'
-lamusha	'awaken'	*-shilika*	'become unconscious, faint'
-many'a	'know'		

Examples of use:

ámiishi ga-kú-py-a	'the water is getting hot'
g-áá-py-a	'the water has become hot'
ga-pí-íle	'the water is hot'
g-aa-pí-ile	'the water was hot' [recently]
índuuny'e shi-kú-ton-a	'the bananas are ripening'; 'they ripen'
sh-áá-ton-a	'they have ripened'
shi-ton-íte	'they are ripe'
sh-aa-tón-ite	'they (had) ripened'
íísuba li-kú-bal-a	'the sun is shining [coming out]'
ly-áá-bal-a	'it has come out and it is bright/sunny'
li-bal-íte	'it is bright/sunny'
li-kaa-lí li-bal-íte	'it is still shining brightly'
a-kw-ííkal-a	's/he is sitting down'
iikííle	's/he is sitting'
iikíile	's/he was sitting'
a-ku-lamúsh-a	's/he is waking up'
aa-lamúsh-a	's/he has awakened'
a-lamush-ííshe	's/he is awake'
a-ku-shílik-a	's/he is fainting'
aa-shílik-a	's/he has fainted/has become unconscious'
a-shilik-íte	's/he's unconscious'
aa-shilík-ite	's/he was unconscious'
	'she fainted' [earlier today]

a-kú-fw-a	's/he is dying/will die'
áá-fw-a	's/he has died'
a-fw-ííle	's/he is dead'
aa-fw-íile mí'masuba	's/he died yesterday'

palá yúmo ááfwa pany'úumba, ábakamu n'abapalámáni
ba-ku-many'-á lubílo
'when someone has died at home, relatives and neighbors
come to know quickly'

n-gú-many'-a ukuti...	'I know [probably, habitually] that...'
n-aa-many'-a ukuti...	'I have come to know that...'
	[= I know now]

palá tw-áá-many'-a ukuti fyúuma
'when we know that it [maize] is dry'

m-éeny'-e ukuti...	'I know [for a fact] that...'
a-yi-meeny'-e iisíla	'he knows the way'

tu-ta-tu-méény'e utusúmo útwiingi 'we do not know many dances'
ngímba umúundu yóo ságula u-mu-méény'e?
'do you know the person who has bought it?'
tu-ta-ba-méény'-e 'we do not know them'

❖ **Stative verbs**

Stative verbs have no internal structure. Rather they indicate a homogeneous state across a temporal domain. Such verbs have the following properties:

- they do not occur in the imperative;
- they do not occur in the *-li pa-INF* construction;
- they have only a habitual or generic meaning with *-ku-*;
- they have a present stative reading in the construction *-Ø...-ite*.

Some verb of this type are:

-beenga	'hate'	*-gana*	'love'
-bona	'see'	*-yaana*	'resemble'

a-mu-beeng-íte	's/he hates him/her'
a-ku-mu-béeng-a	'she hates him' [generally]
aa-mu-béeng-a	's/he has hated him' [e.g., for specific actions]

ifishúuka fi-beeng-an-ité léka n'abáandu bóo balubiile
pakweenda n'úbushiku
'ghosts really hate people who are fond of walking at night'

❖ *-ba* 'be, become'

The verb *-ba* occurs in near complementary distribution with the defective verb *-li* [see following sub-section]. In the indicative, it occurs with all tense and tenor markings. However, with *-ku-*, it has only a generic reading, *-li* being used for present or habitual cases. Both *-ba* and *-li* can occur with anterior *-aa-*, *-ba* giving a dynamic sense of change to a state of being, *-li* simply indicating a state. *-ba*, unlike *-li*, is also used in the non-indicative moods. It may have copular, existential, or possessive uses.

- Copular use

  *ámiishi **ga-ka-ba** mbwée n'ichíisu chóope **chi-ka-bá** chíisa léka kúbulime*
  'water was plentiful and the land, too, was very good for cultivation'

  *usálinjeenti weyóo **a-ku-ba** kubúpiipi n'ipenéenga*
  'the "sargent" is the one who is in close proximity with the *ipenenga* drum'

  *tukubega íchipapa ukuti **chí-b-e** chibúluúnge*
  'we cut the skin so that it is round'

  *bakashaanga palwáala **bú-b-e** búfu*
  'they used to grind [it] on a grindstone [so that] it became flour'

  *indúúmbúla yáangu **tíse yí-b-e** n'úuwé kúúko*
  'my spirit will be with you there'

  *tukukuumbááshe ichibwíina, lóole **chi-tá-ku-ba** chítalí ngááni*
  'we just dig a pit, but it is not a very deep one'

  *liingá aamúbeka umulóonda n'úbwuuki, **t-áa-ka-b-e** mukífu*
  'if he tricked the lookout with honey, he would not be the one who endured pangs [of desire]'

- Existential use

  ***ku-ka-ba** iisála nalóoli* 'there was a lot of hunger'

  *akayá ááwa pachípóso póo **pa-ka-ba** ímwíífwa*
  'she went and fell in a bush on which there were thorns'

  *ímyeenda **yi-tá-ka-báá-ko*** 'clothes did not exist there/then'

- Possessive use

  *mulusáko ulubíibi ubúyo búla **bu-ta-ka-bá** n'ámiishi*
  'unfortunately, that place did not have water'

  ***a-ka-bá** n'ábaana bábili, umulumyáana n'umúliindu*
  'she had two children, a boy and a girl'

104

tw-áá-ba n'úbutolwe múkaaya múno
'we have a problem in this village'

*wéeshi yóo íisa pambúungo **a-ku-bá** n'úbwiigane bwaa kubiikáápo kámu*
'anyone who has come to the funeral has the option to give something'

❖ Defective verbs

• *-li* 'be'

The defective verb *-li* has copular, existential, and possessive functions. In its copular role, it links the subject with an attribute predicated of it or situates it in a location. In its existential role, it indicates what does or does not exist. In conjunction with the particle *n(a)*, it has a possessive function. It occurs either with no tense/aspect marking, or with the anterior marker *-aa-*.

• Copular use

with adjectives or other modifiers

u-li mwáabuke ukuumbá fyóoshi fíifyo waandeendekeshíile
'you are free to give me all that you had planned for me'

tu-li baháano na yúmo twébaana 'we are six, we children'

with nouns

áa-li mwéegi 'she was a married person'

ubwáalwa bwaa Báándali bu-li ulúko píingi nalóoli
'beer of the Ndali people is of many types indeed'

tu-li báana baa bóótaáta béene bóo bakafuma kuTaanzanía
'we are the children of our fathers who themselves came from Tanzania'

with locatives:

b-áa-li kulúsooko 'they were at the river'

a-li kulá n'úmukashi wáake 'he is there with his wife'

amakáto gáá kalulu ga-li pakashíme
'Hare's footprints are by the well'

útááta wáangu a-li palpóónjola 'my father is at Iponjola'

with prepositions

akáboombele káake ka-li ísa kaa mbatáata
'the way of treating them [potatoes] is like that of sweet potatoes'

105

with adverbs:

> *twéeshi tu-li ákiisa* 'all of us are fine'

with ideophones:

> *páase pa-li bísu bísu* 'the floor glistens'
> *chi-li chée* 'it's blood red'

• Existential use

kuMisúuku ku-li ifígaamba léka 'in Misuku, there are many hills'

kuchipíinda ku-li íchiisi 'in the bedroom there is darkness'
[it's dark in the bedroom]

íchaakulyá chóo chi-líí-ko mákoondo géene
'the food that exists there is only coco yams'

• Possessive use

ipenéenga li-lí n'úbwaáshi búkulu nalóoli
'the drum has a very large hole in it'

báti abalóshi ba-lí n'akabíni léka
'they say witches have a lot of jealousy'

tu-lí náa-ki? 'what do we have?'

• Negative

• SP – *tá* – (T/Ten –) *li*

ba-t-áa-li bapíímba 'they were not short'

amahála ga-tá-li n'índaámba 'wisdom does not have a granary'

• SP – *táa*

ichíisu íchi chi-táa chíítu náshiku
'this country of Malawi is not ours [homeland], no'

ísany'aga yi-táa n'ichísa naachímo 'Leopard has no mercy at all'

úutwe twé baana tu-táa n'unáséénge naayúmo
as for us children, we do not have an aunt at all'

• SP – *táa Pfx-N* or *Pfx-Adj*

bataangííkala pamupáando pámu pachitéengu, mwoo lu-táa lu-giindíko
'they cannot sit on a chair or on a stool, which is not respectful'

pakweenda n'úbushiku chi-táa ch-íisa
'to travel at night is not good'

106

• SP – *táa* SP – *b* - *e*

iindámyo shi-**táa** shi-bééko ny'íingi pábwuumi bwáako
'problems will not be many in your life'

• -*ti* 'say, think'

Although a defective verb in terms of the verbal morphology it permits, this verb does occur with the class 15 infinitival prefix, hence, *ukúti*. It can co-occur with the prefixal verb categories (i.e., subject prefix, negative, tense and aspect marking) and with special forms of the suffixal aspect markers, -*ili* [cf. -*ile/-ite*] and -*ingi* [cf. -*aga/-anga*]. It has several uses.

• Quotative marker

bakubuuká kwaa malafyáale pakuyuga ukuti twáába n'úbutolwe múkaaya múno
'they go to the chief saying that "we have a problem in this village" '

úmukashi wáake akati chíisáápo ukubweela
'his wife said, 'it's better to return home" '

umweneng'óombe akati, naatíingi áambééshe ing'óombe sháangu
'the cattle owner said, "I was saying, "he should just give me my cattle" '

móo tukiinong'onélaga tukatiingi títuchípoote
'what we thought was "we will outlast it" '

• Evidential of report

iimbákó shíísho báti shikiipiingílaga
'those caves, they say, used to close themselves'

báti bakayaa pakwiipuuta mukayúumba kála kála
'it is said they used to go to pray in that hut'

• Introducer of ideophones

ngaagááshe iny'áale yááti shimú
'I found the lamp just suddenly went out'
[LIT. it-ANT-ti go-out-suddenly]

• Mental speech

ngatiingi pámu múundu yúungííshe
'I thought it was just a different person'

naatíingi lúmo weyóo aangáye atúsuunge
'I thought that perhaps she was the one who could take care of us'

107

- Complementizer in infinitival form

  *akiinong'ona **ukuti** ááfika kutááwuni*
  'he thought that he had reached the town'

  *ngiinong'ona **ukuti** mwíifi* 'I thought (that) "he is a thief" '

  *ataayúgitéépo **ukuti** úye wíímame mwaa zéenje*
  'he never said that you should go hide in the outhouse'

- Verb of saying

  *uChúungu pakumugela uLwáangwa a-ka-**ti** akaloonda ukumany'á
  liinga uLwáangwa aangába n'amáka gaakupela íifula*
  'Chuungu, to test Lwaangwa, said he wanted to know
  if Lwaangwa had the power to create rain'

108

PART 6

VERBS:
CONSTRUCTIONS AND PHRASES

❖ Simple indicative

• Overview of temporal and modal marking

Simple Indicative constructions consist of a verb base marked for tense, tenor, aspect, and/or modality. The relevant positions of the categories and the possible TMP elements are listed in Figure 6.1 (items in bold obligatory). Other moods, specifically the Presumptive and the Subjunctive, also employ the tense marker *-ka-* and the ASP_2 and ASP_3 elements *-ag-* and *-a-*, hence the discussion of the temporal elements in Indicative forms is complemented with some examples of their use in those moods.

Figure 6.1. Verb template: Indicative

$$\textbf{SP} - TMP - OM - \textbf{BASE} - ASP_1 - VO - ASP_2 - \textbf{F} - ASP_3 = PoF$$

-ka-					*-a* *-a*
-ku-				*-ag-*	
-aa-		*-it-*			*-e*
Ø					
-nga-					

ba-t-aa-fi-lím-it-éé-po
3P-NEG-ANT-8-cultivate-IMPF-F-LOC
'they did not cultivate it [maize] there'

Tense (*-ka-*), tenor (*-ku-*, *-aa-*, Ø), and modality (*-nga-*) markers cannot co-occur in the same verb form. The discontinuous aspect *-it..-e* occurs only with *-aa-* or without any overt TMP marking. The aspect markers *-ag-* and *-a* can occur with all but *-nga-*. The general temporal relation-ship among the construction types is schematized in Figure 6.2. In the future domain, *-ka-...-e* is from the Subjunctive mood template, but in-cluded here to illustrate its complementarity with the Indicative forms. Meanings of the constructions are described in the following sections.

Both for descriptive and analytical purposes, time is represented in two ways: (1) dynamically, in which events are perceived as moving toward the speaker at the time of speaking (S), and (2) statically, in which the speaker moves through time. Consequently, a distinction is made here between tense and tenor, which concern the nature of the temporal relations in terms of these two dimensions. The traditional term TENSE refers to that relation that holds between S (the locus of the speech event) and a temporal reference frame—referred to here as a domain—a relation that is best construed in terms of coincidence. That is, the deictic center (anchored at S) may occur within the time span of the reference frame, i.e., be coincident with it, or it may be non-coincident or exterior to it, in which case the reference frame is labelled as dissociated. In the privileged case of coincidence, i.e., when the temporal reference frame includes S, the reference frame is labeled the P-domain, denoting passing and/or prevailing anterior and posterior relationships to S. For tense relations of non-coincidence, or dissociation, the reference frame is labeled a D-domain. For expository convenience, the different temporal domains (i.e., the different reference frames) are represented as bounded quadrangular planes, as in Fig. 6.2, located along a stationary timeline, i.e., the speaker (Ego) is perceived as moving through time from one domain to another. This contrasts with time represented as moving toward and past the speaker within domains.

Tenor refers to domain-internal temporal relations between an event E and the locus of a reference anchor. This anchor may be the time of the speech event (S), or it may be the time of some other contextually determined event or time.

Figure 6.2. Temporal organization of verb constructions

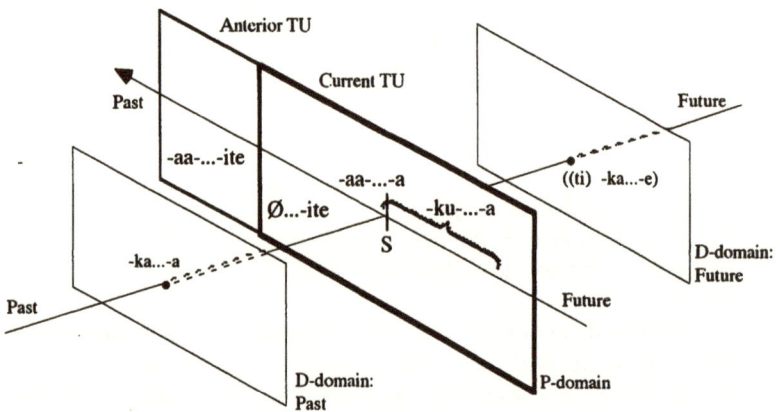

The P-domain is sub-divided into Anterior and Current time units (TU). What this means is that tenor markers, e.g., *-aa-..-a* and *-Ø-..-ite*, refer to some time period earlier in the relevant discourse-established current time unit, for example today, this month, this season, this year. The Anterior time unit will then be interpreted as that comparable relevant time unit, e.g., yesterday, last week, last year.

• **"Remote" past: SP – NEG – *ka* – OM – BASE – *ag – a – a***

The "remote" past, marked with *-ka-*, denotes an event or state that has been projected into the past D-domain. It may have an Imperfective or non-imperfective form, marked by *-ag-/-a* or *-a_F*, respectively. The non-imperfective form is typically interpreted as perfective. The Imperfective forms have habitual or continuous interpretations.

The sense of "remoteness" derives from the dissociated nature of its meaning. Hence, it is commonly associated with events of the distant past, which, because of its systemic opposition to the Completive Anterior, is

112

interpreted as extending from two days ago on. However, it may be used for more recent events if the speaker perceives them as subjectively distant.

With a following complement, the affirmative verb form is all low-toned. Without such a complement, a high-tone occurs underlyingly on the antepenultimate mora. On simple surface forms, the high-tone appears to be on the penultimate mora with monosyllabic stems because the underlying vowel of the root has become a glide. If the negative form, there is invariably a high tone on the negative marker, *-tá-*, regardless of whether or not a complement is present.

SP-**ka**-C(G)-**a**	*chi-ká-w-a*	'it fell'
SP-**ka**-ÓM-C(G)-**a**	*n-gá-chi-ly-a*	'I ate it'
SP-**ka**-ÓM-C(G)-**á ang-a**	*tu-ka-bu-sh-áang-a*	'we used to grind it'
SP-**tá**-**ká**-C(G)-**a**	*ba-tá-ká-lw-a*	'they didn't fight'
SP-**ká**-CVC-**a**	*ba-ká-lim-a*	'they cultivated'
SP-**ka**-ÓM-CVC-**a**	*n-ga-yí-many'-a*	'I knew it'
SP-**ka**-CV́C-**ag-a**	*a-ka-yúg-ag-a*	's/he was speaking'
SP-**tá**-**ka**-ÓM-CVC-**a**	*a-tá-ka-bá-bon-a*	's/he didn't see them'
SP-**ka**-(C)V́VC-**a**	*a-ka-láamb-a*	's/he pleaded'
SP-**ka**-OM-(C)V́VC-**a**	*yi-ka-tu-píimb-a*	'it carried us'
SP-**ka**-CV́CVC-**a**	*tu-ka-hóbok-a*	'we were happy'
SP-**ka**-(C)V́VC-**ag-a**	*a-ka-sééng-ag-a*	'he used to build'
SP-**tá**-**ka**-CV́CVC-**a**	*ba-tá-ka-bónan-a*	'they didn't see e. o.'

Comparable forms with the remote, or PRESUMPTIVE, future are given on pages 132-135, which focus on non-indicative moods, of which the future is a part.

• Simple Anterior: SP – NEG – *aa* – OM – BASE – *ag* – *a* – *a*

The Simple Anterior typically expresses events or states that have just occurred, usually within minutes of speaking. It does not have the experiential sense of the English perfect of having done something at some point in the past, as in *I have been to Malawi*.

Without a following complement, a high tone appears on the antepenultimate mora. With a complement, there is no high tone on the verb except in the negative, where it occurs on the anterior marker *-aa-*.

SP-á á -C(G)-**a**	*y-áá-gw-a*	'it has (just) fallen'
SP-**aa**-ÓM-C(G)-**a**	*aa-tú-kw-a*	'he has paid us [sth.] as dowry'
SP-**aa**-C(G)-**á ang-a**	*y-aa-pw-áang-a*	'it been subsiding'
SP-**t**-á á -C(G)-**a**	*chi-t-áá-py-a*	'it has not become hot'
SP-á á -CVC-**a**	*tw-áá-mal-a*	'we have (just) finished'
SP-**aa**-ÓM-CVC-**a**	*b-aa-mú-piny'-a*	'they (have just) jailed him'
SP-**aa**-CV́C-**ag-a**	*aa-bín-ag-a*	's/he was sick'
SP-**t**-**aa**-ÓM-CVC-**a**	*tu-t-aa-chí-bon-a*	'we didn't see it'
SP-**aa**-(C)V́VC-**a**	*b-éeg-a*	'they have (just) married'
SP-**aa**-OM-(C)V́VC-**a**	*bw-aa-tw-áag-a*	'it has (just) found us'
SP-**aa**-OM-(C)V́VC-**ag-a**	*n-aa-ku-búúl-ag-a*	'I have (just) been telling you'
SP-**t**-**aa**-(C)V́VC-**ag-a**	*ba-t-aa-léémb-ag-a*	'they were not writing'
SP-**aa**-CV́CVC-**a**	*n-aa-púlik-a*	'I have (just) heard'

• **Current Completive: SP – NEG – OM – BASE** – *it* - *e*

The Current Completive refers an event to an earlier time in the current time unit. That is, if the current time unit is "today", the event occurred earlier in the day; if the current time unit is "this year", the event occurred earlier in the year; and so on.

With no following complement, a high tone appears on the penultimate mora. With a complement, there is no high tone present.

SP-C(G)-**í il-e**	*a-mw-iíle*	'he shaved'
SP-C(G)-**í il-e**	*tu-l-iíle*	'we ate [it]'
SP-**tá** -C(G)-**iil-e**	*ba-ta-lw-iíl-e*	'they have not/never fought'
SP-V́V́C-**il-e**	*b-iis-íl-e*	'they have come' [= they are here]
SP-**t**-VVC-**ít-e**	*a-t-eeg-ít-e*	'he isn't married'
SP-CVC-**ít-e**	*a-kam-ít-e*	's/he milked'
SP-OM-CVC-**ít-e**	*a-m-oongesh-iíshe*	'she nursed it'
SP-CVVC-**ít-e**	*tu-byaal-ít-e*	'we planted'
SP-**ta**-CVCVC-**ít-e**	*mu-ta-chi-pulik-ít-e*	'you [PL] didn't hear it?'

114

- **Anterior Completive: SP – NEG –** *aa* **– OM – BASE –** *it - e*

The Anterior Completive refers an event to the preceding time unit. This contrasts with the Current Completive construction that refers an event to the current time unit. The difference between the Current (*-Ø-...-it-e*) and Anterior (*-aa-...-it-e*) Completives can be observed in the following sentence, which contrasts current and anterior time periods. The third sentence illustrates the use of the Simple Anterior.

> *ichíinja ichó chááshila tw-aa-lím-ite ifíloómbe; ichíinja íchi*
> *tu-byaal-ite amálíma*
> 'last year, we cultivated maize; this year, we planted beans'

> *nalóoli tw-[aa-]íínul-a lúluulúúshe* 'in fact, we have just harvested [them]'

A high tone appears on the ante-penultimate mora when the verb has no following complement. With a following complement, there is no high tone on the verb.

SP-**aa**-C(G)-**íil-e**	*y-aa-fw-íil-e*	'it closed' [LIT. died]
SP-**aa**-OM-C(G)-**íil-e**	*tw-aa-shi-l-íil-e*	'we ate them'
SP-**t-aa**-C(G)-**íil-e**	*ga-t-aa-p-íil-e*	'it [water] wasn't hot'
SP-**aa**-V́V́C-**il-e**	*íís-il-e*	's/he came'
SP-**aa**-V́V́C-**it-e**	*n-óóg-it-e*	'I washed'
SP-**t-aa**-V́V́C-**it-e**	*chi-t-úúm-it-e*	'it didn't dry'
SP-**aa**-CV́C-**it-e**	*b-aa-kám-it-e*	'they milked'
SP-**aa**-OM-CV́C-**it-e**	*aa-bu-gán-it-e*	's/he liked it'
SP-**t-aa**-CV́C-**it-e**	*li-t-aa-shím-it-e*	'it didn't disappear'
SP-**aa**-OM-CV́V́C-**it-e**	*aa-m-búúl-it-e*	's/he told me'
SP-**aa**-CVCV́C-**it-e**	*n-aa-ny'amúk-it-e*	'I left'
SP-**t-aa**-CV́V́C-**it-e**	*ba-t-aa-sóóng-it-e*	'they didn't sharpen [them]'

- **Coincident: SP – NEG –** *ku* **– OM– BASE –** *ag – a*

In contrast to *-aa-*, *-ku-* denotes an event coincident with the deictic reference point. It may be (a) on-going (i.e., progressive), (b) habitual, or (c) generic. Note that "present" is a default reading of *-ku-*. If the initial verb of a narrative marks the tense with remote (dissociative) *-ka-*, then subsequent use of either *-ku-* or *-aa-* (i.e., either of the two tenor elements) will be interpreted in the appropriate D-domain. In the samples of the verb construction provided below, only one potential interpretation is given for each example.

As in other simple indicative constructions, a high tone only appears when the verb does not have a following complement, again on the ante-penultimate mora.

SP-**kú**-C(G)-**a**	*tu-kú-ly-a*	'we're eating'
SP-**ku**-ÓM-C(G)-**a**	*a-ku-gá-ng'w-a*	's/he is drinking it'
SP-**ku**-C(G)-**áang-a**	*chi-ku-tw-áang-a*	'it is sprouting'
SP-**tá**-**kú**-C(G)-**a**	*ba-tá-kú-lw-a*	'they don't fight'
SP-**kú**-CVC-**a**	*a-kú-kam-a*	'she's milking'
SP-**ku**-ÓM-CVC-**a**	*ba-ku-bá-many'-a*	'they know them'
SP-**ku**-CV́C-**ag-a**	*ba-ku-líl-ag-a*	'they wail'
SP-**tá**-**kú**-CVC-**a**	*li-tá-kú-sap-a*	'it does not go bad'
SP-**ku**-(C)V́VC-**a**	*fi-k-úum-a*	'it's drying'
SP-**ku**-CV́CVC-**a**	*tu-ku-hóbok-a*	'we are satisfied'
SP-**ku**-OM-CV́V́CVC-**a**	*ba-ku-ba-páángil-a*	'they explain to him'
SP-**ku**-(C)V́V́C-**ag-a**	*shi-ku-kúúmb-ag-a*	'they dig'
SP-**tá**-**ku**-(C)VVC-**a**	*a-tá-ku-káab -a*	's/he does not take long'

• **Event modality: SP – NEG – *nga* – OM – BASE – *a***

The morpheme *-nga-* denotes an event modality. It indicates the speaker's attitude toward the subject's potential to carry out the event named. There are three general uses: Abilitve (indicating the ability to perform the action), the Permissive (indicating that the subject has permission or consent to perform the action), and the Potential (indicating that an event could occur).

A high tone appears on the ante-penultimate mora with no following complement, or on the penultimate if the final consonant is *sh*. No high tone occurs with a following complement.

• Abilitive (Dynamic modality):

*palá aa-**ngá**-pel-a bwoo títúmany'e ukuti nalóoli uyú musúkwa*
'if he can create [it], that is when we will know that, truly, this one is a Sukwa'

*nii-**nga**-hóboka liingá uu-**ngaa**-n-gomólel-a ukáláta úyu*
'I would be happy if you could give me a response to this letter'

*aa-**ngá**-y-e a-tú-suung-e* 'she could [go] take care of us'

*tuu-**ng**-ii-ponésh-a* 'we can save ourselves'

*fy-**iinga**-bá-kol-a* 'they can grab you'

*u-taa-**nga**-ka-tóósh-a* 'you could not defeat him [a mythical little
person]'

116

• Permissive (Deontic modality)

*liingá iitikísha ukuti nalóoli uungamwéega akukubuulá akuti aáma
uungany'éega*
'if she consents that you can marry her, she tells you 'well,
you can marry me'

*akoogopa ukuti wáage aangasééngula muchíllílo íchaa muny'úumba
baangany'ony'a bálye pala iisála yáábaba*
'he was afraid that it was possible if he kept [seeds] in a household
container, they would be tempted to eat [them] when hunger hurt'

muu-ngaa-n-gom-ésh-a 'you can beat me'

tuu-ng-éend-áá-she? 'can we just come here?'

• General potential

bwoo bííkala bakawaaga umútu mwóo ifíindu ífi fii-ng-ééndel-a
'when they had sat [awhile], they found the solution [as to] how
these things could proceed'

*pakuchaaga íchaakúlya yikabá mbóombo yaa kukuumbakuumba
útwaa muchípóso twóo tuu-nga-liil-íw-a*
'to find food, it became the work of digging up little things in the
bush that could be eaten'

tuu-nga-saamil-íbw-a 'they could be transplanted'

❖ **Auxiliary verbs**

• *-ba* 'be'

A construction composed of auxiliary *-ba* plus locative infinitive denotes an
ongoing process. It appears to be limited to the remote *-ka-* construction in the
dissociative past.

   • **SP – *ka* – *ba pa* – *ku* – OM – STEM**

   a-ka-ba pa-ku-lima abóógoóndo 'he was digging potato mounds'

• *-li* 'be' [defective verb]

The construction composed of auxiliary *-li* plus locative infinitive contrasts
with the simple *-ku-* tenor construction. Use of the *-ku-* construction denotes
an internal perspective on the event, hence its use implies that the subject is
actually engaged in performing the activity at the particular time of reference. Use of the *-li* construction, on the other hand, denotes an external view
of the situation, and could be used even if the subject is not, at the time of
reference, actually engaged in the activity but is, for example, taking a break.
The *-ku-* construction might be understood as 'in the midst of', while the *-li*
construction is neutral.

117

- **SP – T –** *li pa – ku –* **OM – STEM**

  a-li pa-ku-mu-liisha úmwaana 'she's feeding the child'

  n-di pa-ku-baamba iiny'áma 'I'm smoking the meat'

  tw-áa-li pa-k-uuba amáshaabala 'we were shelling groundnuts'

  nganíngááni úlwiimbo lúlúúlu ábaana bakwiimbagá palá
  ba-li pa-kw-áángala
  'especially this song children sing when they are playing'

  palá tu-li pa-kw-iimba ichióóta chitiiganíte pakulisha umáliimba
  mwaalwemwáálweeshe
  'when we are performing the chiota dance, one doesn't want to play
  the malimba just any way'

  mwoo a-li pa-k-óótela a-ka-pítila n'ukufwiilá yíiyo kutúlo
  'while he was warming himself [in the sun], he fell asleep and
  died in his sleep'

- **Perstitive** *-kaa-li*

Perstitive is a cover term for three constructions related by their use of the
form *-kaa-li*. Two of the constructions incorporate an infinitive as complement, either the bare infinitive (*u-ku*-Stem) or a locative infinitive (*pa-ku*-
Stem). These constructions give the sense of 'not yet' (literally, 'yet to Verb').
The semantic difference between them remains unclear.

- **SP –** *kaa – li u – ku –* **STEM**

  mwoo a-kaa-li u-ku-ny'ámuka akayá aabálaga usékulu n'úmaáma
  'before he had yet set off, he went [and] bid farewell to grandfather
  and grandmother'

  palá a-kaa-li u-ku-sayíwa akwaanda ichipímo kuchípataala
  'when she is yet/still to be blessed [i.e., to give birth], she starts
  prenatal care at the hospital'

- **SP –** *kaa – li pa – ku –* **STEM**

  palá bakukuumba ipúumba ínga baalyáaga ííbwe lyaalite páase,
  báti umúundu umúfwe yúla, bwoo a-kaa-li pa-kú-fwa, ashilikité búubu
  'when they dig the grave and find a big rock embedded on the bottom,
  they say that dead person, it means s/he is not yet dead [LIT. yet to die],
  s/he is just unconscious'

  mwoo ba-kaa-li pa-ku-mwiita úmwaana bakweega ubulíli
  bakumugóneka,
  'at the time they are yet/still to name the baby, they take a sleeping
  mat [and] lay it [baby] down'

118

The sense 'still' is imparted when the complement of -li is inflected for person and tenor. A diffence in time of the event—present versus past—is manifested by a difference in tone on the auxiliary— -kaa-lí for present, -káa-li for anterior—arising from a difference in tenor marking: -Ø-kaa-li versus -aa-kaa-li, respectively, with tone assigned accordingly to the con-struction.

a-**kaa-lí** a-ku-kam-a ulúkama	's/he is still milking milk'
aa-**káa-li** a-ku-kam-a ulúkama	's/he was still milking milk'

Negation of the complement denotes a sense of 'not yet'.

- **SP – kaa – lí** SP – NEG – Ten – **BASE – F**

utusúmo túmo **tu-kaa-lí tu-kw-iimb-á** núulu
'some dances we still perform even now'

soóna mupáka núulu góogo mugúunda **ba-kaa-lí ba-kú-lim-a**
'also until even now, it is in that field that they still cultivate'

pakabalílo áka ukupíímbila **ku-kaa-lí ku-shaalikiile** mutubúyo túmo
'at this time, betrothing a child is still practiced in some places'

íísile ááfwa **a-kaa-lí a-ku-yug-a** ichiNy'akyúusa
'he eventually died still speaking Kinyakyusa'

n-gaa-lí n-gw-iitee ndekésh-a ukuti mbwéele
'I am still preparing myself to return home'

úmukolo
liingá a-lí n'ulufúkwe,
liingá **a-kaa-lí a-t-oog-íte**
ínga úmukolo yúúyo mupáapi wáá mwaana yúuyo **a-kaa-li** ukuti
á-kul-e,
úmwaaná yúúyo lúmo akúfwa

'a woman,
if she is pregnant [LIT. has a belly],
if she has not washed yet [i.e., had a menstrual cycle],
and the woman is the parent of a child who is yet that s/he grow up,
that child may die'

The construction takes on a past interpretation when it occurs in a sub-ordinate clause and the matrix clause is in the past.

boo **a-káa-lí a-ku-kuut-á** kúla kúla, abáandu batákabá náfyo
n'imbóombo
'since she was still wailing at that very place, people did not care'
[LIT. have things with task]

119

tu-kaa-lí tu-ku-yugiisanyá n'uNáambene, abáandu bakaanda
pakwíika
'[as] we were still talking to each other, Nambene and I, people started
to get off'

tu-kaa-lí tu-kw-iinóng'ona, úmukolo yúla akaany'iitísha
'[while] we were were still thinking, that woman called me'

akaanda ukulibulanya ichípaanga chíla n'ifikókwe mupáka pakakiinda
usambáata a-káa-li
'he began digging up that cave with big sticks until there passed a week
[and] he was still [at it]'

• Aktionsarten

Various Aktionsarten are expressed through auxiliary verbs that refer to a particular phase (or sub-phase) of an event. They occur in constructions in which
the auxiliary occurs in an Indicative or Presumptive form followed by the
main lexical verb in either bare infinitival form (hence, *u-ku*-Stem) or infinitival form preceded by locative *pa*- (hence, *pa-ku*-Stem). The difference is
approximately equivalent to the difference in English between *start Verb-ing*
and *start to Verb*.

-ya 'go'

Auxiliary *-ya* contributes a sense of initiating an action at a pre-inceptive
phase. Compare this with auxiliary *-iisa* which denotes a post-terminative
phase. Both *-ya* and *-iisa*, unlike other Aktionsarten, permit the main verb to
be in non-infinitival form.

• SP – T – *y* – F *pa-ku*-STEM

n-gu-y-a pa-ku-seenga kwIpóónjóla 'I am going to build at Iponjola'

ábaana bíitu báabo tu-ku-y-a pa-ku-páapa táa bátwaage utusúmo
naatúmo naatúmo
'the children that we are going to bear will not find any of these dances'

palá ku-ku-y-a pa-kú-cha, bakukuba ipéenga
'when day [goes to] break, they beat the ipenga drum'

nguloondá ń-j-e pa-ku-loonda imbóombo yóoshi yóo naayáaga
'I want to go to look for any job that I [can] find'

• SP – T – *y* – F *ku* – STEM = PoF

umúundu yóo a-kw-iis-a ku-yugá náwe weyóo a-ku-y-a kw-eegiwáá-ko
'the person who finally talks with her is the one who is going to
marry her'

120

-ny'amuka 'set out' [about to]

This auxiliary denotes a perspective at the initial onset phase of the event as the actor is about to engage in the action.

- SP – T – *ny'amuk* – F *pa-ku*-STEM

   fyóo ny'amuk-it-e pa-ku-siimba pánu fyaa kukwaafanyánífyaa pákaaya
   'what I am about to write here relates to our home'

-aanda 'start/begin or set out'

Auxiliary *-aanda* has two related uses. It may denote an aspectual perspective either (1) at the initial onset of an event, as the activity gets underway, or (2) at the beginning of the characteristic nuclear phase of the event.

- SP – T – *aand* – F *u-ku*-STEM

   bakiimbagá mupáka aboobíísa b-áand-e u-k-úúbika
   'they performed until roosters began crowing'

   ba-k-aand-a u-ku-buukililá n'ubuléendo bwáabo ukuyiilá kwaa Túúnduma
   'they set out continuing with their journey, going through Tunduma'

- SP – T – *aand* – F *pa-ku*-STEM

   liingá áand-a pa-ku-mela ámiino, uung'ína a-kw-aand-a pa-ku-mu-liish-a ubugáli
   'when s/he has started to teethe, her/his mother starts to feed her/him bugali'

   usékulu akatí aabóomba ifyíinja kalóongo, a-k-aand-a pa-kú-bina
   'after Grandfather had worked for 10 years, he began to get sick'

   tukweega ifíloómbe tukubiika mukáti mukásefulila; poo tu-kw-aand-áang-a pa-kú-kuba
   'we take some maize [and] we put [it] inside a small pot; then we begin to beat [it] [= play]'

-leka 'stop, cease; quit'

Auxiliary *-leka* denotes a cessation of activity. In the construction with the bare infinitive, it implies complete discontinuation of the activity with no sense of resumption. With the locative infinitive, it has a more neutral sense, resumption possible.

- SP – T – *lek* – F *u* – *ku* – STEM

   kwookuti ápa gw-áá-lek-a u-ku-lya kuny'úumba yaa bapáapi báako
   'it means that now you quit eating in your parents' house'

   lóole ápa amábwe ága ga-ka-lek-a u-kw-ííguka
   'but now those rocks have quit opening themselves'

- SP – T – *lek* – F *pa* – *ku* – STEM

   aa-lék-ite pa-kú-kama 'she stopped milking' [earlier today]

   ábagome bóoshi bá-lek-e pa-ku-lipila ísoóngo
   'elderly people, all of them, should stop paying taxes'

-buukilila 'continue'

Auxiliary *-buukilila* denotes continuation of the characteristic phase of the event with or without a pause in the activity.

- SP – T – *buukilil* – F *u-ku*-STEM

   uné n-ga-buukilil-á n'u-ku-mu-buula ukuti ...
   'me, I even continued telling her that...'

- SP – T – *buukilil* – F *pa* – *ku* – STEM

   a-ka-buukilil-a pa-kú-yuga akáti...
   's/he continued to speak, saying ...'

-mala 'finish, complete'

-mala denotes the final phase of an event. With a bare infinitve as complement, it simply indicates a perspective at the end of an event. With the locative infinitive, it implies that a certain wholeness to the activity that has been achieved.

- SP – T – *mal* – F *u* – *ku* – STEM

   boo áá-mal-a u-kú-lya, akati shutú
   'when he had finished eating, he suddenly turned his back and left'

   pala usékulu akabáápo, ngali tu-ka-mal-a u-ku-lima umugúunda
   'if grandfather were here, we would have finished cultivating the field'

- SP – T – *mal* – F *pa* – *ku* – STEM

   palá tw-áá-mal-a pa-kú-sha tukwaata iny'dambo
   'when we have completed grinding, we make [beer] wort'

   liingá b-áá-mal-a pa-ku-shíila poo usóongo waa chádliki chíla chíla akuluumbílila
   'if they have completed burying, then an elder of that church preaches'

122

-iisa 'come'

Auxiliary *-iisa* contributes a sense of arriving at or reaching a particular state or condition, equivalent in English to 'come to', 'finally', 'ultimately'. As with *-ya*, it permits a non-infinitival complement or a bare infinitive without the augment.

- **SP – T – *iis* – F SP – T – BASE – F**

  a-k-iis-á áá-fw-a ubúkaangale 'he finally died of old age'

  a-k-iis-á aa-séeng-a iny'úumba yáake kúkaaya kóo ílyiita koo kwiPóónjóla
  'he ultimately built his house at the village which is called Iponjola'

  aáma akalaambá mupáka b-íis-a b-aa-tóond-a indúúmbúla
  'well, he pleaded until they finally "softened [their] hearts"'

  n'uutwé tw-íis-e tw-iigúlil-e alílage poo tumógage
  'we, too, will come to turn [it] on [so that] it will be making sounds so we will dance'

- **SP – T – *iis* – F *ku* – STEM**

  umúundu yóo a-kw-iis-a ku-yuga náwe weyóo a-ku-y-a kw-eegiwááko
  'the person who finally talks with her is the one who is going to marry her'

• **Action sequencing**

Auxiliaries of this type indicate the sequencing of actors or actions, or the repetition of actions, either intermittently or repetitively.

-aanda 'be first'

- **SP – T – *aand* – F *u-ku*-STEM**

  weyúuyo a-k-aand-a u-ku-fika kúno
  'he is the one who was first arriving here'

-taanga 'do sth. first'

- **SP – T – *taang* – F SP – T – OM – BASE – F**

  uúkabwa akamusuuma úkalulu ukuti agáángule ifiny'ámáana fyóoshi fyóo fikutamiwá n'utuséénga múmaaso; úkalulu akíítika poo a-ka-taang-á aa-mu-gáángul-a úúkábwa
  'Dog begged Hare to heal all the animals that were suffering from little grains of sand in the eyes; Hare accepted, so he first healed Dog'

  tu-táang-e tw-áá-ly-a bwoo tutabuukíte kumugúunda
  'we should first have eaten before we go to the field'

123

-kaambe 'do again' [defective verb—only used in the negative sense 'never ever']

- **SP** – *kaamb* – *e* **SP** – **OM** – **BASE** – *e*

    *many'é **mú-kaamb-e** mu-ny'óókel-e kuTanzanía*
    'don't you ever again return to Tanzania'

-pyaanisha 'repeat (an action)'

- **SP** – **T** – *pyaanish* – **F** *u-ku*-**STEM**

    ***aa-pyaanish-íishe** u-ku-puula ifíloómbe*
    'she again pounded the maize'

-bona 'see'

- **SP** – **T** – *bon* – **F** **SP** – **TEN** – **OM** – **BASE** – **F**

    ***a-ka-bon-á áá-kul-a** akaanda isukúulu mu wáanu*
    'having grown, he started school in first grade'

    ***a-ka-bon-á aa-mú-p-a** umuléembo aamubúúsha ukuti babééshe
    -kúla kúla*
    'having gaven him medicine, he told him that they should just stay there'

    *akiisá aapáapa úmwaana umúliisha yóo **a-ka-bon-á áá-kul-a**
    akaba mwíifi*
    'he came to bear a male child who, when he grew up, became
    a thief'

• **Conative expressions**

Auxiliary *-ti* 'say', a defective verb, may function to express the attempt to do something which does not, in fact, occur. The intercalation of *íse* into the construction appears to emphasize the robustness of the attempt.

- **SP** – **T/Ten** – *ti* (*íse*) **SP** – **OM** – **BASE** – *e*

    ***a-ka-ti íse a-pékes-e** munó ná muno aapóótwa*
    'he tried his best to make a fire; [but] he failed'

    a-ka-ti á-kol-e, *áaga bóoshi baakíinda*
    'he tried to catch [them], he found they all ran away'

    ***tu-ka-ti tu-liindílil-e** tukapóótwa*
    'we waited in vain' [LIT. we tried we waited we failed]

    *boo **a-ku-ti á-y-e pa-kw-áámula***, *akaaga imbíingu yikwáángala
    múny'oobe*
    'when he tried to (go to) answer, he found handcuffs (playing)
    on his hands'

124

• Auxiliary *-ti* 'say' as referential index

As an auxiliary, *-ti* often functions as a referential index, denoting a second reference point (R2) with respect to which the event is temporally located. The T marking on *-ti* indicates the temporal relation of this R2 to the speech event (S), the primary reference point. Marking on the main verb indicates the relation of the event to R2.

Indicative constructions

• SP – T/Ten – *ti* – F SP – Ten – BASE – F

íifula yi-ka-tí yi-kw-íis-a yikakuusa ifibyáálibwa fyáabo
'when the rain came, it damaged their crops' [remote]

a-ka-t-iingí aa-gulísh-a asoongélage ifíisi kusukúulu
'after having sold [pots], she paid the school fees' [remote]

ba-ka-tí-í ba-kw-aabuk-a ulúsooko, bakaponyaa íinguku múmiishi
'each time as they crossed the river, they threw a chicken in the water' [remote]

b-aa-tí ba-kw-aambuk-a ulúsooko, bakawiiláámo
'as they were crossing the river, they fell in'
[earlier today or yesterday]

tu-ti-il-í tw(-aa)-ííkal-a, poo tu-áánd-ag-aang-a pakuyugílana
'after we had sat down, we then began negotiating'
[earlier today or yesterday]

a-ku-tí-í a-ku-kam-a ulúkama, úmulume akusukaga utúpáále
'usually when she milks (milk), her husband cleans gourds
[for storing it]'

Presumptive constructions

• *tí* – NEG – *se* SP – *ti* – ASP SP – Ten – OM – BASE–F

tí-n-di n-aa-líísh-a ing'óombe, tímbweelage
'after I graze the cattle, I will return home' [later today]

tí-tu-tí-i tw-aa-mú-bon-a, títukííndage
'after we see him, we will run away' [today or later]

tí-ba-tí-i ba-ku-mú-bon-a, tíbakiindage
'every time we see him, we will run away'

tíse tu-tí-i tu-kalal-íte, tíse tukaáane pakumwaafwa imbóombo
'whenever [each time] we have become angry, we will refuse to help him with work'

tíse tu-tí-i tw-aa-líísh-a ing'óombe, tíse tuyaange kulúsooko pakóoga
'whenever [each time] we have grazed the cattle, we will go to the river to bathe'

- **Propositional and event modalities**

  - **Necessity**

The speaker's judgment of a proposition as necessarily or logically the case is indicated by the auxiliary *uku-bagila*.

  - **SP – NEG – Ten – *bagiile u-ku* – OM – STEM**

    a-bagiile u-ku-yi-many'a iisíla 's/he must know the way'

    bakakaanganá léka nábo mupáka bakiinong'ona ukuti
    wíini a-bagiile u-ku-ba malafyáale waa chíisu chaa Misúku
    'they quarreled a lot with each other until they decided
    who ought to be the chief of the land of Misuku?'

    bakuloondá bakwaatíshe páapo bati ubukwáati bukunósha pakuti
    ifíindu fímo bakukupá fyóo u-t-aa-bagíile u-ku-fyáaga
    'they simply want to wed because they say a wedding is interesting
    since some things they give you (are things that) you must not have
    gotten [otherwise]'

    Non-auxiliary use:

    ichikókwe chi-bagiile ukuti chi-b-áang-e pyáa
    'the wood must be very smooth'

    umáliimba a-bagiile ukuti a-b-áang-e n'isáambo éiti
    'the *marimba* must have eight metal keys'

  - **Obligation**

The following two auxiliary particles express the speaker's attitude toward the future occurrence of an event, in these cases one of obligation.

  - **íse: *íse* SP – OM – BASE – *ag – e***

This auxiliary particle derives from the verb *-iisa* 'come'. It is used either literally to indicate motion to a deictic center, as in the first two examples below, or to indicate temporal motion toward an event, as in the remaining examples.

    naatumíwa ukuti íse n-gulísh-e iiny'áma
    'I have been sent so that I should (come to) sell the meat'

    bakamupimila umulumyáana íishiku lyaakuti íse a-komáan-e
    n'aboogwíise
    'they determined for the young man a day that he should come
    meet with the fathers'

    bwíila úbubine bwaa múundu múkaaya bukupulikikwá táashi ínga
    íse mu-pulík-ag-e ubúfwe bwáake
    'usually a person's illness is known in the village first and then
    you (come to) hear of his death'

126

bakupamaandá búubu panáandi ukuti many'é íse bu-sáátan-é
   ngááni
'they just pat them [sesame seeds] gently so that they should not
(come to) scatter all over'

n'úune íse m-bámany'-e 'and I, I should (come to) know them'

akuyaangááshe mupáka íse yi-kwaan-e náyini
'she just keeps going [to the hospital] until nine [months] should
(come to) pass'

ábaana n'aboowíise bakagonaa pamúpééne mpáka íse bá-fik-e
   pakabalílo káá bweegi
'children and parents used to reside together until they [children]
should (come to) reach the time for marriage'

• *íye*: *íye* SP – OM – **BASE** – *ag* – *e*

Similar to *íse*, *íye* is derived from a motion verb, *-ya* 'go'. However, it
appears not to be as common in use. Only the following example of literal
motion has been discovered.

umalafyáale akubabuula ukuti íye ba-kúut-e imbúungo
'the chief tells them that they should (go to) announce the funeral'

❖ **Non-indicative moods**

There are four non-indicative moods in Chindali: imperative, subjunctive,
presumptive, and exhortative. They are distinguished both by form and by the
manner of negation.

• **Imperative**

The imperative can be formed on the bare radical with final *-a*, but it may be
more typical to have final *-aga*. Some verbs, like *-bweela* 'return home' may
be used only in the *-aga* form. This form occurs only in second person, with
no distinction in form when addressing singular or plural persons.

• Imperative template

   NEG   IT – OM – **BASE** – ASP – F = PoF

   kóoma ka-   *-ag-*   *-a*
                                            -e

teshá mwóo bakufugila ubugáli   'watch how they make bugali'
yuungaanya umuléembo   'shake the medicine'
leka pakubelebéeta   'stop babbling!'
komelá ámiishi gaakumwooshela úmwaana
'cool the water for bathing the baby'

127

| *lim-ág-a* | 'hoe' |
| *bweel-ag-a kukwíiny'u* | 'return home to your place' |

Monosyllabic stems add *-ang-* to form the simple imperative.

| *ly-aáng-a íchi* | 'eat this' |
| *mw-aáng-a* | 'shave' |

The verb *-iisa* 'come' has special forms, *saa* or *isaa*.

| **saa** *kúno* or **isaa** *kúno* | 'come here' |
| **sáá** *náfyo ífyaa kwiimbila kúno* | 'bring [LIT. come with] the [music] playing things here' |

When the imperative verb takes an object, the verb adds an agreement prefix and changes final *-a* to *-e*.

mw-íifwiing-e úmwaana	'cover the baby'
tu-p-e indaláma	'give us money'
gu-golósh-e	'straighten it [line].'

The prefix *ka-* has an itive function. Added to the imperative, it expresses movement away from the deictic center, i.e., away from the speaker's location. It also appears to indicate metaphorically movement into the future.

ka-mu-bíík-e 'go and show him (e.g., house)'

k-eeg-e aboomáánga mumugúunda waa pákaaya
'go and get pumpkins from the garden near the house'

ka-chi-seengul-e ichíindu ícho, túkiimbage níngeelo
'go [ahead] and keep that thing, we will dance tomorrow'

• **Negative of the imperative**

The negative of the imperative is formed from *kóóma* (variant *kwoóma*) plus the class 15 infinitival form of the verb. Typically, in speech, *kóóma* elides with the following infinitive therby losing its final vowel.

kwoóm(a) ukúlya 'don't eat'

liinga úmwaana ataabóomba imbóombo kóóm(a) ukumupa ubúlye
'if a child has not worked, don't give her food'

kóóm(a) ukubalekela ábakolo imbóombo shóoshi shaa pákaaya
'don't leave all the housework for women to do'

kóóm(a) ukuya pakumulámuka, báti mulóshi léka
'don't go to greet her, they say she is really a witch'

poo ichí bakakaanisha aboosóongo; bakati indagílo shímo
*tubábuushdá tdáshi bwoo tutaboombíte, **kwoóm(a) ukufulúúngana***
'so elder people forbid this; they said some things we should ask them
first before we do them; don't rush'

• **Subjunctive**

The subjunctive occurs with all persons as subject. It is formed in the
affirmative with stem-final -*e* and a high tone on the ante-penultimate mora,
unless followed by the enclitic -*she* 'just', which requires a high on the
preceding vowel. Although it is required in many subordinate clauses, it also
occurs in main clauses.

• Subjunctive template

NEG   **SP** – T – OM – **BASE** – ASP – **F** = PoF
many'e   -*ka*-   -*ag*- -*e*

• Directive function

úu-n-dap-e! '[you SG] leave me out of it!'

w-íis-e u-gólok-e nagúu muséébo
'[you SG] just [come and] go straight on the road'

n-áand-e n'ipenéenga 'I should start with the *ipenenga* dance'

tu-táang-e twáálya 'we should first eat'

u-búuk-e pakuubula ing'óombe 'you [SG] should go skin the steer'

áa-m-b-éé-she ing'óombe sháangu 'he should just give me my cattle'

liingá akushílika, ú-mu-p-e umuléembo úgu
'if s/he faints, you [SG] should give her/him this medicine'

akamupepeeka ukuti a-búuk-e náwe
'he persuaded her that she should go with him'

bakapaangana ukuti ba-ḳomáan-e sóóna
'they agreed that they should meet again'

úlwiiba lu-fwéén-ag-e lwiilíkila pámwaany'a
'the grass should look like it had covered the top'

ubúyo bwóo tukúsala bú-b-e kúpiipi n'ímishitu
'the place that we choose should be near forests'

• Weak directive function

tu-kú-tuul-e 'may we/I [polite] help you [SG]'

iínga ngweegíwa, mu-ly-áang-e íchuuma, náákula
'yes, I am getting married; you may receive the dowry, I am an adult'

129

múú-siimbil-e ukuti m-bá-liingaany-é bwíísa
'you [PL] should write me in order that I may explain [them] to you well'

fímo ngubapa ábakamu báangu báabo mbabuulite ukuti
mú-k-iis-ag-e pakwáángala
'some I give to my relatives whom I have told saying "you should come to chat" '

- Jussive function

  n-gu-loondel-e kámu káako kakusalasala pánu
  'let me look for a certain one [young woman]'

  tu-yá-ban-e íchuuma 'let's share the wealth [livestock]'

  tw-éend-e tubwééla 'let's go home'

  tw-éend-e tú-kit-e 'let's go do [it]'

  tu-móg-ag-e iing'óma 'let's perform the ing'oma dance'

  ka-lek-é ka-y-áang-e 'let him [the little guy] go'

  aáma shi-lek-é shaa cháala 'well, let it be, it's of God['s will]'

- Future function

  - Coincident future: **SP** – OM – **BASE** – *ag* – *e*

    íchaakuti m-bá-buul-e chaakuti liingá...
    'what it is that I will tell you is that if...'

    ...ukuti íifula yi-w-áang-e ákiisa '...so that it would rain well'

    bakabaamba ábakolo béene, abáliisha béene, poo
    ba-komáán-ag-e pakáti
    'they stood in line, women only and men only, then they would meet in the middle'

    akafiinga ukuti mpáka á-mu-kol-e úkalulu
    'he promised that, no matter what, he would catch Hare'

    utúbwe túla tukang'anamula ukuti mány'e umúfwe yulá
    á-b-iisil-ag-e kutúlo
    'the small stones meant that the dead person would not come for them in their sleep'

    pala ífyuulu fyaabwéela bakapalíla ínga ba-kupíkil-e n'ámaani
    gáá nduuny'e
    'when anthills had developed, they scraped [them] and then would cover [them] with banana leaves'

130

báti ifúundo íingulu yóo bakaloondelaa ukuti úlwiiba luyáa
mutúsakasa twáabo báti yikabá yaakuti ing'óombe shíla báti
shi-ly-áa na pábushiku múla múla
'they say the main reason why they wanted the grass to go into
their huts was that the cattle, they say, would eat in there even at night'

- Dissociative future: **SP** – *ka* – **OM** – **BASE** – *ag* – *e*

tu-k-iimb-ag-e níngeelo 'we will dance tomorrow'

mú-k-iis-e íishiku ilyaakuti mu-ká-komaan-e n'aboogwíise
'you [PL] should come on a day on which you [PL] will meet with
the fathers'

ú-k-iis-ag-e n'ing'óombe 'you [SG] will come with a cow'

liingá aakolíwa mú-kaa-m-b-e úne
'if he has been caught, you will give him to me'

• Itive function of -*ka*-

The marker -*ka*- can function to indicate movement away from the deictic
center, as in the Imperative. This may be physical or "temporal" movement.

n-g-éeg-e aboomáánga mumugúunda waa pákaaya
'I should go get pumpkins from the garden near the house'

many'é mu-ká-saamil-ag-e naakúmo soóna, mwée baa kuMisúku
kúno kúno mupáka mú-ka-fw-e
'don't you [PL] go move anyplace again; you are from right here
in Misuku until you [go and] die'

• **Negative subjunctive**

The negative subjunctive is formed from *many'é* plus the subjunctive form of
the verb. The negative force of the utterance appears to depend on the context,
ranging from a strong directive 'don't' to milder 'shouldn't' or 'needn't'.

*tiiláako, **many'é** mu-palamíl-ag-e pápiipi*
'move away; don't [you PL] come near'

***many'é** mu-bákol-ag-e mútukono*
'don't [you PL] touch them on the hands'

***many'é** u-ká-puluusany-e ulúsooko*
'don't [you SG] go crossing the river'

***many'é** u-mú-sekel-ag-e úseéle*
'you [SG] shouldn't laugh at hammerkop'

***many'é** mw-éénd-ag-e n'akáfweleléma*
'you [PL] shouldn't walk in the dark'

131

mubóombe ífyaakúti, fímo **many'é** *mu-bóomb-e, mwíiko!*
"you [PL] should do such-and-such, some things you should not do,
ever!'

many'é *mu-lóónd-ag-e úmwaana wíiny'u*
'you [PL] needn't look for your daughter'

ámashika ága abáandu báanda pakúlima ukuti **many'é**
ba-tamiw-áang-e n'iisála
'these days, people have started to cultivate so that they need not be
afflicted by hunger'

ámiisa bakoongaanyá n'ílyooto ukuti **many'é** *ga-fukwáang-e*
utufúkwe
'the good ones [beans] they mix with ashes so that they won't become
full of weevils'

bakééta ifíkuúbi **many'é** *fi-kól-ag-e íinguku*
'they watch for chicken hawks [so that] they won't catch chickens'

Note, also, that in one case, the negative verb prefix -*tá*-, rather than
many'é, occurred in the subjunctive construction.

*palá tuungagáaga ámiishi, úkalulu a-**tá**-kaa-ng'w-éé-po shíku*
'if [assuming] we can find water, Hare should never drink [it] ever'

• **Presumptive**

The Presumptive mood indicates that the speaker takes for granted that the
event is reasonably likely to occur. It expresses the event as future and, hence,
as yet to be verified. The body of the construction—that beginning with the
subject prefix (SP)—has the same structure as the subjunctive (q.v.), Although
similar to the subjunctive, the construction differs in that the negative is formed
with the prefix -*a*- in the auxiliary element. It differs from the Indicative
template both in the use of an auxiliary proclitic element and in the obligatory
final vowel -*e*, indicating the non-actuality of the mood.

tí – NEG – *se* **SP** – TMP – OM– **BASE** – ASP – **F** – ASP = PoF

    -*a*-   -*ka*-   -*ag*- -*e* -*aa*

• **Simple Presumptive futures**:

ti- constructions: *tí* – *a* **SP** – *ka* – OM – **BASE** – *ag* – *e* – ASP = PoF

The morpheme -*ka*-, as noted elsewhere, indicates subjective remoteness
of an event as projected into a future D-domain. Without -*ka*-, the event is
inter-preted as occurring within the P-domain. The configuration *ti* ...-*e*
denotes high probability, in the speaker's judgment, of the occurrence of an
event in relatively close proximity to the speech event (S) (Figure 6.3). In

contrast, the configuration *ti -ka-...-e* places the event in a dissocated domain, suggesting less certainty or confidence on the part of the speaker that the event will actually occur.

Figure 6.3. Presumptive futures

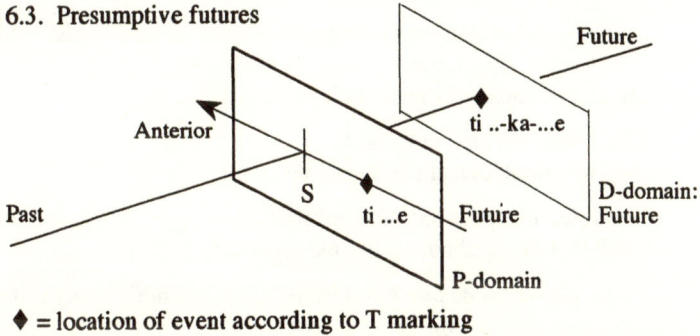

♦ = location of event according to T marking

The Presumptive futures, with or without *-ka-*, have an invariable high tone on the initial proclitic *tí-*. A high tone may appear on the ante-penultimate mora if there is no complement following the verb. With a following complement, there is no high tone.

tí-ŚP-C(G)-e	*tí-tú-fw-e*	'we will die'
tí-SP-ÓM-C(G)-e	*t-a-chí-ly-e*	's/he will eat it'
tí-SP-C(G)-áang-e	*tí-ba-ly-áang-e*	'they will be eating'
táa ŚP-C(G)-e	*táa bá-y-e*	'they won't go'
tí-SP-CVC-e	*t-á-kam-e*	's/he will milk'
tí-SP-OM-CVC-e	*tí-ba-tú-many'-e*	'they will know us'
tí-SP-OM-CV́C-ag-e	*tí-m-ba-kól-ag-e*	'I will be catching them'
táa SP-CVC-e	*táa bá-yug-e*	'they won't talk'
tí-SP-(C)V́VC-e	*tí-b-íis-e*	'they will come'
tí-SP-OM-(C)V́VC-e	*tí-tu-chi-póoɬ-e*	'we will defeat it'
tí-SP-CV́CVC-e	*tí-mu-púlik-e*	'you [PL] will hear'
tí-SP-CVCV́C-ag-e	*tí-yi-ny'amúk-ag-e*	'it will be taking off'
táa SP-CVCVC-e	*táa tu-pulíkan-e*	'we won't get along together'
tí-SP-ká-OM-CVC-e	*tí-tu-ká-ku-tumy-e*	'we will send for you'
tí-SP-ká-CVVC-e	*tí-n-ga-fwiil-e pánu pánu*	'I will die right here'
tí-SP-ká-OM-CVVC-e	*ɬ-ú-ka-tú-shiil-e*	'you [SG] will bury us'
tí-SP-ká-VVC-ag-e	*tí-n-g-aand-ag-e ibíízinesi*	'[then] I will start a business'
táa SP-ka-OM-VVC-e	*tá-a-ká-mw-aag-e lúmo úmukolo*	'he would never find a woman'

133

tí-n-aand-e n'umútu waa múumwo abáándali bakweegela iny'éega
'I will start with the topic of how the Ndali people perform marriages'

*ndi n'úbwaa nalóoli ukuti aáma **ti-tú-fi-many'**-e fyóoshi*
'I am sure that, well, we will know everything'

*umútu gwáá bubili **tí-gu-kwaafány'**-e n'íshaa múumwo abáandu bakufyaagila ífyaakúlya*
'the second topic will relate to how people find food'

***tí-ba-t-íingi** wii múkaa múundu*
'they will think that she is someone's wife'

***tí-n-júg-aa** ichi pálwááke ichi pálwááke*
'I will be talking about each topic separately'

***táa-tu-búuk-e** péene póo íifula yikúwa* 'we will not go only if it rains'

***táá-n-jug-éé**-po íny'iingi pandóófáni ísho*
'I won't say much about those potatoes'

*ábaana bíitu **táa-bá-tw-aag-e** utusúmo naatúmo naatúmo útu*
'our children will not find any of these dances at all'

- **Presumptive indexed futures**: *tí – a – se* **SP** – *ka* – **BASE** – *e*

The *tise* configurations indicate that the occurrence of an event depends on the occurrence of some other event. The auxiliary element *se* indexes a second point of reference (R2), which acts as a new locus of orientation, having, like S, two perspectives on time (see Fig. 6.4). The event proper is then interpreted with respect to the occurrence of the event or condition denoted by R2. As with the simple presumptive futures, the marker *-ka-* situates the event in a D-domain.

Figure 6.4. Presumptive indexed futures

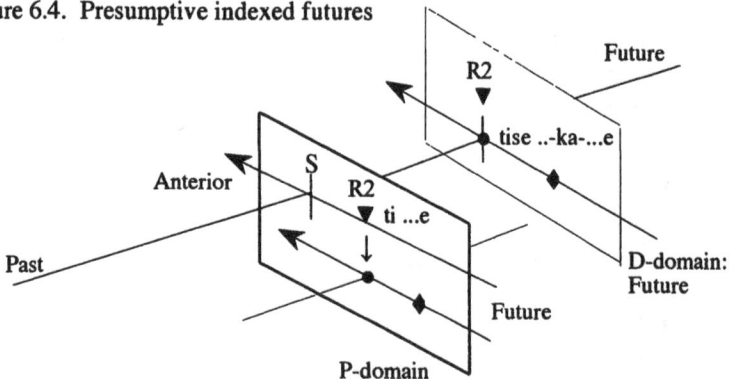

♦ = location of event according to T marking
R = reference time of some indexed event

tí-se ŚP-C(G)-e	*tí-se yí-b-e n'úuwé*	'it [spirit] will be with you'
tí-se ŚP-OM-C(G)-e	*tí-se á-tu-p-e*	'she will give us [sth.]'
tí-se SP-C(G)-**áang-e**	*tí-se tu-y-áang-e*	'we will go'
t-áa-se ŚP-C(G)-e	*t-áa-sé ń-j-e*	'I will not go'
tí-se ŚP-CVC-e	*tí-se yí-ny'al-e*	'it [cow] would be filthy'
tí--se ŚP-OM-CVC-e	*tí-se bá-tu-bon-e*	'they will see us'
tí-se SP-CV́C-**ag-e**	*tí-se a-kám-ag-e*	'she will be milking'
t-áa-se SP-CVC-e	*t-áa-se bá-gul-e*	'they will not buy [it]'
tí-se SP-OM-V́VC-e	*tí-se á-b-oosh-e*	'she will wash them'
tí-se SP-CV́VC-e	*tí-se ba-tíim-e*	'they will graze [them]'
tí-se SP-CV́CVC-e	*tí-se tu-sékel-e*	'we will celebrate'
tí-se SP-CVCV́C-**ag-e**	*tí-se tu-pulíkish-ag-e*	'we will be listening'
t-áa-se SP-CVVC-e	*t-áa-se bu-kwáan-e*	'it will not fit'
tí-se SP-ká-C(G)-**aang-e**	*tí-se tu-ká-ly-aang-e*	'we will be eating'
tí-se SP-ká-OM-VVC-e	*tí-se a-ká-mw-eeg-e*	'he will marry her'
tí-se SP-ká-OM-CVVC-e	*tí-se n-ga-kú-paangil-e*	'I will tell you'
t-áa-se SP-ká-CVVC-e	*t-áa-se ba-ká-loond-e*	'they will not look for [it]'

*pala úmwaana aapaapíwa, **tí-se tu-sékel-e***
'when the child is born, we will celebrate'

***tí-se n-gú-buulil-e** kwáá taáta* 'I will report you to father'

***tí-se tu-sukúsul-e** palá twáámala imbóombo*
'we will wash when we finish work'

akápaango kaa báándali liingá tuuti tukokotéshe kóoshi fweení
***tí-se tú-mal-e** amapéépála ámiingi léka*
'as for the story of the Ndali people, if we try to tell all, it seems we
might use up a lot of paper'

*palá sháába shéene, bakiinong'onaa ukuti **tí-se yí-ny'al-e** léka nóo*
waa kuyipúúpula
'when they [cattle] were alone, they used to think a cow would
suffer without anyone to clean it up'

***t-áa-se ń-j-e** kuMaláawi ichíinja ichó chikwíisa, náálita léka n'ífyaa*
kweendakwéenda
'I will not go to Malawi next year; I'm too tired with traveling'

*ubúfu búubu **t-áa-se bu-kwáan-e** muchindundúúnga chíla, bwíingí lúkulu*
'this flour will not fit in that basket; it's too much'

*palá utákuchiseengula ákiisa, **tíse ba-ká-loond-e** bapóótwe*
'if you do not keep it properly, they will look and look [for it] [and]
will not find [it]'

135

The difference between the presumptive futures and the futurate use of the Subjunctive is very subtle and as yet remains unclear. The following example illustrates how one speaker has used both in a single sentence. It appears that the Subjunctive expresses a higher probability in the speaker's judgment than does the Presumptive form.

> *liindilila indaláma shóo **tí**-m-bokéél-**ag**-e kubumalílo bwáá mweeshi shóo n-**gá**-ba-p-e mwééndele mwíígali*
> 'wait for the money that I will be receiving at the end of the month which I will give you [so that] you travel by car'

As a final note, the proclitic *ti-* appears in a variant form as a particle *ití*:

> *ití **mu-púlik-e** íshaa basúkwa* 'you will hear about the Sukwa people'

• Exhortative

The Exhortative is a combination of imperative *sáá* 'come' plus the subjunctive form of the verb.

> • Exhortative template

$$\textbf{\textit{sáá}} \; \text{SP} - \text{OM} - \textbf{BASE} - \text{ASP} - \textbf{M}$$
$$-ag- \qquad -e$$

> **sáá** *tu-yá-ban-e íchuuma cháá tááta chíicho akatugulila kuTaanzanía*
> 'come, let's share the livestock that Father bought us in Tanzania'

> *mwaabíika imíindu pany'úumba yáangu,* **sáá** *mu-tíísh-e*
> 'you have made a mess at my house; come on, just remove it'

> **saá** *m-ba-tum-e kumasitóolo* 'come, let me send you to the stores'

> • Variant: *isáá*

> *báleesha,* **isáá** *tu-kíínd-ag-e* 'gentlemen, (come) let's run'

❖ Adverbs

Adverbs constitute a large open grammatical class. Although there is no single morphological characteristic common to all adverbs, many are formed productively by reduplication or derivation using locative prefixes, *pa-* or *mw(aa)-* in particular. Common examples are categorized following below.

• Manner

Manner adverbs typically derive from adjectives, e.g., *ák-iisa* < *-iisa* 'good', or verbs, e.g., *chí-mye* < *uku-myeeka* 'to be quiet'.

136

ákiisa	'well'
bwíisa	'well' [to a suitable or appropriate degree]
chímye	'quietly'
lubílo	'quickly'
pálwááke	'separately, by itself'
ububíibi	'badly'
mwáálwe	'by any means'
mwaalwemwáálwe	'any old way, haphazardly, carelessly'

mwaakuchéétwa	'late'	[mw + aa + ku.VERB STEM]
mwaakufikísha	'adequately, satisfactorily'	
mwaakufwáasa	'contentedly'	
mwaakwiilómuka	'in a sloping manner'	
mwaakukwaanísha	'in a fitting manner'	
mwaakwiikwéésha	'boastfully'	
mwaakunósha	'in an interesting manner; comfortably'	
mwaakoogófya	'in a scary or frightening manner'	
mwaakutamíwa	'uncomfortably'	

• Intensifying

Intensifying adverbs are often derived by reduplication of another adverb.

akisákíisa	'very well'
bwiisábwíisa	'very nicely, thoroughly'
chimyémye	'very quietly'
lubilolubílo	'very quickly'
léka	'a lot, hard'
ngáani	'a lot'
nganíngáani	'really, especially, mainly'
panáandi	'a little bit'
panaandipanáandi	'gradually'
lúkulu	'to an extreme, too much' [of some measure]

• Spatial

kúno	'here'
kúno kúno	'right here'
múno	'here inside'
pánu	'here'
pánu pánu	'right here'

137

- **Temporal**
  - **Time**

kuuny'úma úkwo	'in the past'
kále	'long ago'
iyólo	'some time ago'
ichíinja ichó chááshila	'last year'
úmweeshi úgo wááshila	'last month'
usabáata uyó áámala	'last week'
lútaashi	'2 days ago'
m(ú)masuba	'yesterday'
úmuusúgu	'today'
níngeelo	'tomorrow'
usabáata úyu	'this week'
úmweeshi úgu	'this month'
ichíinja íchi	'this year'
usabáata uyó akwíisa	'next week'
úmweeshi ugó gukwíisa	'next month'
ichíinja ichó chikwíisa	'next year'
pángeélo	'morning'
pámúúsi	'midday; afternoon'
námasuba	'evening'
úlu	'now'
ápa	'now/at this time'
ápo	'then/at that time'
popáapo	'right then and there'
nakálíínga	'at once, immediately'

  - **Frequency**

shíku	'(n)ever'
lúmo	'(n)ever'
kámu	'once'
mutubalílo	'sometimes'
bwíila	'often'
piipípíípi	'frequently'
pápiipi pápiipi	'very often, frequently'

- Other

ngaani	'already, in advance'
nganííshe	'in advance'
pakátaashi	'later'
paany'úma	'later'

- Focusing

búu	'just, only'
búubu	'even, just'
soóna	'also, too'
n'úulu	'even now'
n'úulu búubu	'even now, already'

- Qualifying attitudes

káli	'perhaps'
lúmo	'perhaps, maybe; sometimes'
pámu	'perhaps'
mulusáko	'luckily, fortunately'
ngíimba	'unknowingly'
nalóóli	'in fact, truly'

PART 7

IDEOPHONES

❖ General features of ideophones

Ideophones constitute a distinct grammatical category whose lexical items may serve to emphasize the extreme nature of the concept modified or the suddenness of the action. Common semantic themes are sound, color, texture, gait, other movement, breakage, and scintillation. In addition to the inherent members of this category, others are derived from verbs, adjectives, or nouns.

Ideophones are commonly short words (see Table 7.1), typically one or two syllables, often reduplicated. In some cases, they may be pronounced in unusual ways, e.g., whispered, or with an accompanying gesture.

Table 7.1 Common ideophone types

CV	*pya*	'absolutely empty'
CV	*ndwí*	'quick, strong, sudden grasping'
CVV	*tii*	'stink to high heaven'
CV́V	*swée*	'snow white'
CVCV́	*bwinú*	'of suddenly falling over backwards'
CV́CV CV́CV	*kápa kápa*	'dripping wet'

[C = C, C^w, C^y, ^nC, $^nC^w$]

Although ideophones may be used in a variety of ways, they typically occur with one of four verbs: *-ba* or *-li* 'be', *-aaga* 'find', *-ti* 'say'. Examples of these are provided below, with both the verb and ideophone in bold.

-li	**ubuutité uli búu**	'you are dusty to the point of griminess'
	páase pali bísu bísu	'the floor glistens'
-ba	ichikókwe chibagiile ukuti **chibáange pyáa**	'the wood must be smooth as glass'
	úmaáyi **áábaáshe myée** nóo kwáámula	'mother was just quiet without speaking'
-aga	úkalulu **áaga ndwí** bamukolíte	'Hare found that "zap" they had caught him'
	ngaagááshe mulí	'I found [it] just flickered and went out'
-ti	fyaatííshe **páasi sáa**	'they just fell and scattered helter-skelter'
	bóoshi bííkala ifyéeni **fyááti télatéla**	'all sat solemnly, heads bowed'
	akeendá akatíingi **chápa chápa**	'he walked quickly, going swoosh, swoosh'

143

Other examples:

*íínguku shikafwa **pípipípi***	'the chickens died, every last one'
*naany'amúkite pángeélo **pwíi***	'I left in the morning at the crack of dawn'
*aalíile íchaakúlya chóoshi **pyáapyaápyaa***	'she completely ate up all the food'

❖ Categories of ideophones

Ideophones may be categorized according to the sensual or motional qualities they express.

• *Color*

chée	'deep red'
fíi	'jet black'
swée	'snow white'

• *Sound*

chwí	'light, squeaky sound'
fyáá	'expression to scare away chickens'
kee.	'sound of tearing'
pwaa	'sound of shattering plate, glass'; 'clapping'
chuumbwí	'of falling in water kersplash'
palakáta	'sound of eerie rustling'
cháka cháka	'sound produced in shaking'
pwáa pwáa pwáa	'sound of clapping, formal and in unison'
tó tó tó tó	'of the sound of water dripping'

• *Texture*

pyáa	'of being smooth as a baby's bottom'
swée	'of being squeaky clean'
syée	'of being very flat and smooth, like glass'
twáa	'of being very hard, rock solid'
wáá	'of the sound made by hitting or slapping an ear with the open palm'
kápa kápa	'dripping or soaking wet'

144

• *Smell*

tii	'of having a very strong odor, stinking to high heaven'

• *Body and gestures*

bwáashi	'bare-naked'
nguule	'buck-naked' ·
ndwí	'quick strong sudden grasping'
téla téla	'with heads bowed'

• *Gait*

chápa chápa	'of walking quickly'
pínu pínu	'of walking in a way that is considered pretty for girls to walk, i.e., 'shaking her bottom'

• *Exhaustive*

fwáa	'full to the brim'
mbwée	'plentiful, abundant'
myáa	'consume completely'
pya	'of sth. that is completely empty inside, all used up'
pyáapyaápyaa	'completely'
kámu kámu	·'absolutely nothing'
pípi pípi	'die out completely or end completely, time and again, frequently'
pípi pípi	'of lying so much that one cannot believe a word s.o. says'

• *Miscellaneous*

bwinú	'falling over backwards suddenly'
geletú	'appear or arrive suddenly'
pwíi	'crack of dawn'
sáa	'of being spread out, scattered'
toputóopu	'of having a good time, enjoying oneself'

❖ Ideophones derived from verbs

Derivation of ideophones from verbs is a highly productive process in Chindali. Typically the final syllable of the verb stem is deleted; the vowel [u] may replace the vowel of the new stem.

• *Color*

sweepú	'of suddenly becoming white'	<	*-sweepa*	'become white'

• *Sound*

cháku cháku	'sound of chewing'	<	*-chakuusha*	'chew noisily'
bulukútu	'sound of heavy things falling'	<	*-bulutuka*	'fall [of heavy items]'
fúlu fúlu fúlu	'sound of rapid boiling'	<	*-fulukila*	'boil'
gúchu gúchu	'sound of eating sth. hard'	<	*-guchula*	'chew under-cooked yams'
koongómo	'of laughing heartily'	<	*-koongomoka*	'laugh jovially'
myée	'of being very quiet'	<	*-myeeka*	'be quiet'

• *Sudden movement*

fukutú	'sudden quick movement'	<	*-fukuta*	'move'
fumi	'of coming out suddenly'	<	*-fuma*	'come out'
iimú	'of suddenly stopping dead in one's tracks'	<	*-iima*	'come to a stop'
lekú	'stop suddenly'	<	*-leka*	'cease, stop'
ny'amú	'of getting up quickly/suddenly'	<	*-ny'amuka*	'get up'
palasú	'of scratching suddenly'	<	*-palasa*	'scratch'
shutú	'of leaving suddenly'	<	*-shuutuka*	'turn one's back'

146

• Falling

bulutú	'of falling like a heap of heavy things'	<	-bulutuka	'fall [of heavy items]'
lapatú	'of falling gliding in the air'	<	-lapatuka	'fall, gliding in air'
telegú	'fall making a sound'	<	-teleguka	'fall from usual place'

• Walking gait

gombóto gombóto	'lazily'	<	-goombotoka	'walk lazily'
kapátu kapátu	'heavily with ponderous steps'	<	-kapatuka	'walk heavily'
loombóto loombóto	'in a slow, lazy manner'	<	-loombotoka	'walk in slow manner'
pembénu pembénu	'unsteadily, as if drunk'	<	-peembenuka	'walk unsteadily'

• Texture

bísu bísu	'oily in appearance'	<	-bisuka	'be or appear oily'
búu	'extremely dusty'	<	-buuta	'be dusty'
lilímbu	'of being stretched out'	<	-liliimbuka	'be sticky, stretched'
lipwití	'soft as silk'	<	-lipwitika	'be soft'

• Breaking/ripping

balú	'split suddenly'	<	-baluka	'split in two'
begú	'break suddenly'	<	-beguka	'break off'
ng'wápu ng'wápu	'of slashing through sth. quickly'	<	-ng'wapulanya	'do sth. quickly'
putú	'of breaking in half suddenly'	<	-putuka	'break in two'
satú	'of sudden ripping at seams'	<	-satuka	'rip at seams'

• *Scintillation*

mulí	'of flickering quickly and suddenly going out'	<	*-mulika*	'twinkle'
múli múli	'twinkling'	<	*-mulika*	'twinkle'
mwetú	'flash suddenly'	<	*-mwetuka*	'flash'
shimú	'of going out suddenly'	<	*-shima*	'become extinguished'

• *Miscellaneous*

kúli kúli	'of gulping a drink'	<	*-kuliisha*	'gulp'
mákolele	'of holding on w/o letting go'	<	*-kolela*	'hold'
pénu	'of a door being wide open'	<	*-penuka*	'be wide open'
piikapíika	'of lying much and often'	<	*-piikapiika*	'lie often'
téte téṭe	'tremble with fear'	<	*-tetema*	'tremble, shiver'

❖ **Ideophone derived from an adjective**

bísu bísu	'not fully cooked'	<	*-bisi*	'raw, uncooked'

❖ **Ideophone derived from a noun**

makamáka	'strong, powerful'	<	amá.ka	'strength'

PART 8

SYNTAX

❖ Basic word order: S-V-PO-SO-OO

The basic word order in simple indicative sentences is SVOO, with the primary object preceding the secondary object, followed by any oblique objects.

> *úkalulu akamutiisha*   *uúkabwa utuseséénga*   *múmaaso*
> 1.hare   1.RM.1.remove_from   1.dog   13.grains_of_sand   in.6.eyes
> 'Hare removed from Dog's eyes small grains of sand'

> *bakamupimila*   *umulumyáana íishiku lyaakuti íse   akomáane*
> 2-RM-1-determine-APP-F   1.young_man   5.day   5.that   come 1-meet-SUBJ
>
> *n'aboogwíise*
> with-2a.fathers
>
> 'they determined a day for the young man to come meet the fathers'

> *bakamulaangaga umúliindu umúundu yúuyo   akuloonda ukumwéega*
> 2.RM.1.show.IMPF 1.girl   1.person   1.1.REL   1.CO.want   15.1.marry
> 'they showed the girl the person who wanted to marry her'

The goal may follow the secondary object, but it then requires a locative prefix, for example, *ku-*.

> *ábakamu báake   bakutuma íindumi   kúmafumu*
> 2.relative   2.3S.POSS 2.CO.send-F 9.message 17.6.chief
> 'his relatives send a message to the chiefs'

❖ Alternative word orders

In many instances, alternative word orders occur in which either the subject or the object is located in a different position from that observed above in the basic word order. These alternative orders represent discourse strategies connected with the presentation or introduction of new entities into the discourse, focus on these entities, or topicalization.

• V-S order

Verb – subject order appears to serve three functions in Chindali: (1) to introduce a new entity into the discourse, what can be designated a presentational function; (2) to introduce a new subject (i.e., switch from a previous one); or (3) to place focus on the subject.

• Presentational constructions

In presentational constructions (similar in form to existential constructions, see pages 178-179), the nominal entity being introduced into the discourse narrative follows the verb, typically *-li* or *-ba* 'be, exist' but others as well, and agrees with it. In each example below, the presentational construction is in bold.

151

ákapote lwíimbo lwóo tukwiimbaga kumulómu; **ba-kw-iimb-aga**
abáandu bábili.   2-CO-perform-IMPF
  2.people

'*akapote* is a song that we perform through the mouth; [there are]
two people [who] perform [it]'

fi-lii-kó fímo *ifiyúni bakutukaanila pakúlya*
8.exist-17 8.some 8.birds
'there are some birds we are forbidden to eat'

shi-lii-kó shímo *íinjoka bakuti abóóchipili*
10.exist-17 10.some 10.snakes
'there are some snakes they call puff-adders'

li-ka-báá-ko límo *iikókwe lyóo bakatii mwíiko pakukéenda*
5-RM-exist-17 5.certain 5.tree
'there used to be a certain tree which, they said, was taboo to cut down'

tukaya pakuliindilila íígali poo twíisa twáaga ísa líigi twáaga
ly-áá-fika íígali
5-ANT-arrive 5.car

'we went to wait for a car; so we came to find after some time we
found it arrived, a car'

liingá **kááfika** *akabalílo kaa kweeganílana, umúliisha akutuma*
         12-ANT-arrive 12.time

   umúfuusha

'if the time has come for them to marry, the man sends his
representative'

ka-k-iisa *akabalílo kámu káako bakaanda pakubeenganá*
12-RM-come 12.time

   beenébééne

'there came a time when they started hating each other'

Notice in the example that follows the complex informational structure in
which the presentational construction occurs. The backgrounded place—
Masukulu—against which the new, foregrounded information, *masuku* fruit,
is presented, represents old information and, consequently, is sentence-initial.
Furthermore, the new entity is presented in the context of the general topic
'main food'. (See discussion of topic prominence that follows.)

*paMásukulu íchaakulya íchikulu **ga-ka-bá** **masúku*** *gáago gakabá*
        7.food   7.main   6-RM-exist 6.suku_fruit

míingi nalóoli

'at Masukulu, [as] main food, there was *masuku* fruit, which was plentiful'

• Switch or introduction of new subject

An unexpected switch to—i.e., the introduction of—a new subject, is often expressed by placing the subject in typical object position following the verb. The subject noun still determines agreement on the verb. That this position is salient can be observed in the first two examples below, describing aspects of maize and bean production. Following a long description of maize/bean culti-vation in which he uses 'we' and 'they' as subjects, the male narrator then switches to women, who are the agents of the activities mentioned, shelling maize and pounding it, in the first case, winnowing beans in the second.

palá mukuloonda ukulya ubugáli, mukweega ifílóómbe, mukupaany'a
    *imíindu; palá baapáany'a imíindu, **ba**-ku-bulul-a **ábakolo**, báasi*
    bakukóbola   2-CO-shell-F   2.women

'when you want to eat *bugali*, you take the maize [and] you remove the husk; when they have removed the husk, women shell [it], then they pound [it]'

tukwiimbagá péene páchaaka na pachilísimaasi; úlwiimbo lúluulu
    ba-kw-iimb-agá   nganíngááni ábaana abakéke
    2-CO-perform-IMPF   2.children 2-young

'we perform [it] only at New Year and Christmas; this particular song mainly young children perform'

pambúungo yaa sékulu bakiimbagáápo íny'iimbo ngáti íshaa búsaamba;
    *lóole poopé shitákahoboshaangá ngáti shíisho **ba**-k-iimb-aa*
    ábaa chipáanga   2-RM-perform-IMPF
    2.LNK 7.church

'at the funeral of Grandfather, they [non-Christians] sang songs like *busamba*; but, even so, they [songs] were not as interesting as those chúrchgoers sang'

• Subject focus

V–S order may also serve to indicate focus on the subject, as illustrated in the examples below.

palá giinulígwa tukubá twéeshi pamúpééne abáliisha n'ábakolo;
palá twáákuba, **bakugulusha ábakolo**
                        2.CO.winnow 2.women

'when they [beans] have been harvested, we beat them, all of us together, men and women; when we have beaten them, [it is] the women [who] winnow them'

umúfuusha akubapa indaláma abóómáyi; pabumalílo bakuti úkiise
sóóna lishiku ilíingi liingá kááfika akabalílo, **a-ku-pyaanil-á** *sóóna*
umúfuusha *pakuyugiisanyá n'aboowíise*   1-CO-negociate-F again
1.representative

'the marriage representative gives money to the mothers; finally, they say you should come again another day; if the time has come, [it is] the representative [who] returns again to negotiate with the fathers'

ámashiku ága ficheenjíte; **ba-ku-sal-iw-á**   **bámu**   *páluko* *bóo*
                      2-CO-choose-PASS-F 2.certain 16.11.clan

   bakupokeelaga ámakiba

'these days things have changed; [it is] certain ones in the clan [who] are chosen to receive the offerings'

úlwiimbo lúluulu bakwiimbagá nganíngááni ábaana abakéke;
'this particular song mainly young children perform.

   loole kutaa kwookuti **bakwiimbaga**   **beene abaana** **abakeke**,
                      2.CO.perform.IMPF-F 2.only 2.children 2.young

   but it does not mean that [it is] only young children [who] perform;

   nashiku **bakwiimbagaashe**   *n'aboosoongo pala biigana*
          2.CO.perform.IMPF-F-just even-2.elders

   ukwiimba, poo bakwoongaana n'abakeke

   no, [it is] even adults [who] perform if they want to, so they join with the young'

Focused subjects may also occur in sentences in which there is an initial topicalized noun. (See also section on Topic prominence that follows.)

*ábakolo **yi-ka-b-aang-áá-she mbóómbo** yaa kupiiya íchaakúlya*
9-RM-be-IMPF-F-just   9.work

n'ukuya pakubashiindika ábalume báabo kumigúunda
'women, [their] work was just to cook food and to take it along to their
husbands in the fields'

* **O-V order**

Object–verb order serves two functions: (1) to focus the object, or (2) to
topicalize the object.

* Object focus

An object in a clause in which there is no nominal subject can be put into
focus by shifting it to a pre-verbal position, Such focus constructions pre-
suppose that some entity has experienced the action denoted by the verb, and
assert that the object noun is that entity.

amálíma palá baagulúsha, bakuseba ámiisa,
'beans, when they have winnowed [them], they pick out the good ones;

*góo **mabíibi** bakupiiya,*
the ones that are bad they cook,

ámiisa gála bakubiika mumasáaka bakoongaanyá n'ílyooto
those good ones they put in a sack, [and] they mix with ashes'

ifyíina ífi   bakakuumbilagá   chóo tukuti ichisopéko
8.holes 8.these 2.RM.dig.APP.IMPF.F
'these holes they dug using what we call a *chisopeko*'

ulwiimbo ulu tutakwiimba mwaalwe nashiku
'this song we do not sing at just any time, no'

nganíngááni úlwiimbo lúlúúlu bakwiimbagá palá bali pakwáángala
'mainly, this particular song they sing when they are playing'

* Object topicalization (internal)

An object may also function as a clause-internal topic by shifting it to
clause-initial position (see the section on Topic prominence below for a discussion of clause-external topics). Often the topicalized object co-occurs with
a focused subject that (1) either follows the verb or (2) occurs in copular form
(i.e., without the augment and with high tone shift if the high tone was on the
augment).

_____TOPIC_____
iny'uumba yaake   *akuseenga kumakokwe kumwaany'a.*
9.house   9.3S.POSS 1.CO.build.F
'its house [nest] it [hammerkop] builds at the top of trees'

                               __TOPIC____
liingá twáámoga ichipaláano, ímyeenda yíla   tukusééngula yaa
   kumogelá sóóna   4.clothes 4.those 1P.CO.keep.F 4.LNK
      15.dance.in

'if we have danced a competition, those clothes we keep for
dancing in again'

___TOPIC_____
akápaango áka *many'é mutíi néene n'ímweene naaléemba*
'this story,   do not think [that] I alone have written [it]'

___TOPIC_____   ___FOCUS_____
ulwiimbo luluulu   *bakwiimbaga nganingaani abaana   abakeke*
11.song   11.paricular 2.CO.perform-F mainly   2.children 2-young
'this particular song mainly young children perform'

TOPIC   _____FOCUS_____
ichiméle ba-k-iimb-ag-a   *abéegi n'abakéenja   búubu*
7.dance   2-RM-perform-IMPF-F 2.married and.2.unmarried even
'the *chimele* dance married and even unmarried people used to perform'

_TOPIC__   _____FOCUS_____
ingúúmbe a-taa-nga-piiy-a   *uung'ína waa kámwaana yúla*
9.pot   1-NEG-POT-heat_to_boil-F 1a.mother

      liinga akámwaana káfyééle

'a pot she was not able to heat up [i.e., not able to cook], the mother of
that baby, if it was [still] newborn'

                     _____TOPIC_____ _FOCUS_
liinga úmukolo íita ukátoote, yúuyo aamukóonga ukátoote múliisha
   akwíita

'if a woman named the first-born child, the one who follows the
first-born child, it is the man [who] names'

- Modifier focus: **S-V-MOD**

A modifier such as a number or quantifier can be placed in focus by placing
it in a position away from the noun it modifies. Thus, it may be moved away
from a subject noun to a position following the verb, or it may remain alone
following the verb in an existential construction while the noun is moved to
topic position.

156

*umufúúngula úwaa nduuny'e gúugo **abáandu** bakuny'amulaga **bátatu**,*
                    2.people   2.CO.carry.IMPF   2.three

úmwééne akany'amulagá mwééne

'a stalk of bananas which 'three people usually carried,
he himself carried alone'

*ámatone n'íísugu shikakupuká **shóoshi***
'the bananas and *isugu* peas spilled out, all [of them]'

❖ Topic prominence

In Chindali narrative, especially, speakers commonly organize sentences, or clauses therein, in terms of a topic and a comment on that topic. These topics are external to the structure of the sentence. They differ from clause-internal topics (see previous discussion) in two ways: (1) objects that are topics must have an object marker on the verb, and (2) external topics often seem completely independent of the comment sentence. Topics are typically the first element in the sentence or clause, but may be preceded by adverbial elements or locatives. There may be more than one topic in a sentence.

- Subject topicalization

____TOPIC_____ _____COMMENT_____
ifíshiinga fyáá ngwi ífíkulu palá fikwáaka aáma ifíloómbe fíla fikuuma ákiisa
'large pieces of firewood, when they burn, well, that maize dries well'

        __TOPIC___ __.____COMMENT_____
*soona **useele yuuyo** mwoo akugona mwiisa leka.*
'also that hammerkop, where it nests is very nice'

- Object topicalization

____TOPIC_____ ___COMMENT_____
indagílo shóoshi íshi úkalulu akashímany'a
'all these rules,   Hare knew them'

                                        __TOPIC__
*chikabá cháá chitima léka pakupulika ukuti **uNáambene***

     ___COMMENT___
íinjoka yaamúlúma

'it was very sorrowful to hear that,   Nambene,
a snake had bitten her'

• General topicalization

TOPIC _____COMMENT_____
imótóka abáándali batákashimany'a pakále
'cars,   the Ndali people did not know about them in the past

__TOPIC_____ _____COMMENT_____
iny'úumba shóope abáándali batákashímany'a íshaa málata
'houses, also,   the Ndali people did not know of iron roofs'

__TOPIC_ _____COMMENT_____
íchaakulyá bakatupiiyila ízuumba poo n'ubugáli bwaa nachíleenje
'[for] food, they cooked for us okra and *bugali* made out of millet
flour'

__TOPIC__ _____COMMENT_____
ichipóonde bakoongaanya imbatáata n'amálíma
'*chiponde*,   they mix together potatoes and beans'

                TOPIC _____COMMENT_____
ukufuma ápo úkalulu   ámiishi gatákamalikaa lúmo páapo

_____
    akaseengulagá góoshi góo gakwíisa

'from then on, Hare,   water never ran out because he stored all the
    water that came'

• Double topicalization

    __TOPIC___ ____TOPIC___ ____COMMENT_____
poo ífyaakulya ífi akálimile káake táa kwookuti bakulimila

    pakabalílo kamúkééne náshiku'

'so, these foods,   their cultivation, it does not mean that they grow
[them] at the same time, no'

❖ **Primary and secondary objects**

Chindali contrasts primary and secondary objects. Primary objects are either
patients (objects of simple transitive verbs) or goals (of ditransitive verbs).
They may trigger agreement on the verb or be passivized. Secondary objects
(themes of ditransitive verbs) do not permit either.

ba-ka-mu-tum-a uWaamahála íchaabúpe
2-RM-1-send-F 1a.Wamahala 7.gift
'they sent Wamahala a gift'

uWaamahála a-ka-mu-tum-iw-a íchaabúpe
        1-RM-1-send-PASS-F
'Wamahala was sent a gift'

158

*a-ka-**chi**-tum-a uWaamahAla
* *íchaabúpe* chi-ka-mu-tum-iw-a uWaamahála
*a-ka-chi-tum-a *íchaabúpe* kwaaWaamahAla

*a-ka-**li**-p-a **íibwe** íingamu*
'she gave the rock a name'

a-ka-mu-p-a úmaáma ululagílo
'he gave grandmother a rule'

  *akalupa úmaáma
  *ululagílo lukamupewa úmaáma
  *akalupa ululagílo kwaa maáma
  *akalupa úmaáma

*tu-ka-**mú**-seeng-el-a uNjéki iny'úumba kwiPóónjola*
'we built a house for Njeki at Poonjola'

  *uNjéki akaseengelewa iny'úumba kwiPóónjola
  ‾ *iny'úumba yikamuseengelewa uNjéki kwiPóónjola
  *tukayiseengela uNjéki

*umúliisha a-ku-**mu**-p-a umúliindu ichikóole*
'the man gives the woman a token of engagement'

umúliindu a-ku-p-ew-a ichikóole n'umúliisha
'the woman is given a token of engagement by the man'

  *umúliisha akuchipa umúliindu
  *ichikóole chikumupewa umúliindu n'umúliisha

❖ **Object agreement marking**

Object agreement marking on the verb denotes the definiteness of the nominal reference.

  • Definite reference

*ba.ka.**ba**.poota ába.lugu bá.la*
2.RM.2.defeat 2.enemies 2.those
'they defeated those enemies'

yúmo umukúumbi akwiisá   alíbuule   íifumu ilyoosóongo
1.one 1.digger 1.CO.come 1.5.tell.SUBJ 5.chief 5.elder
'one of the diggers comes [*and*] tells the head chief'

159

aamúbeka   umulóonda n'úbwuuki
1.ANT.1.trick 1.lookout   with-14.honey
'he tricked the lookout with honey'

abáandu baamutúútite   léka úmwiifi
2.people 2.ANT.1.beat_hard very 1.thief
'people beat the thief very hard'

[anthropomorphized object]

úkalulu akang'oombola úbwuuki n'ukuyimyaasha   ínjeeye
1a.hare 1.RM.scoop   14.honey and.15.9.lick.CAUS.CMPL 9.crab

   mumulómu
   18.3.mouth

'Hare scooped up some honey and made Crab lick [it] in its mouth'

[object agreement with non-animate]

palá tukayimany'a iisíla, ngalí twaabúuka
when 1P.RM.9.know 9.path then   1P.ANT.go
'if we knew the way, then we would/could go'

abáandu ábiingi batákayigana isukúulu
2.people 2-many 2.NEG.RM.9.like 9.school
'many people did not like school'

• Indefinite reference, hence, no object agreement on the verb:

baabíika umulóonda pakashíme
2.ANT.put 1.watchman 16.12.well
'they had put a watchman at the well'

liinga umulumyáana akuloonda ukwéega, akuloonda   umúliindu
when 1.young_man 1.CO.want 15.marry 1.CO.look_for 1.girl
'when a young man wants to marry, he looks for a girl'

ichipóonde bakoongaanya imbatáata n'amálíma
7.chiponde 2.mix   10.potatoes and-6.beans
[for] *chiponde*, they mix together potatoes and beans'

aboong'ína   bakugula ingúúmbe n'imbáale
2a.her_mothers 2-CO.buy 9.clay_pot and-10.crockery
'her mothers buy a clay pot and crockery'

bakabegaga amákwaamba ágaa fitíindi   n'amásakata gaa
2.RM.cut.IMPF 6.bark   6.LNK 8.banana_trees and-.6.leaves 6.LNK

   kumuteengeláápo úmwaana
   15.1.lay_on.16   1.child

'they used to cut bark and dry leaves of banana trees to lay
the child on'

160

BUT:

ábiingi bakeegelela üsíla yáake íyaa   kuseengulila ümbeyu
2.many 2.RM.copy 9.way 9.his 9.LNK 15.keep   10.seed
'many copied his way of keeping seeds'

akaboná bóoshi baapítila   *poo apiny'iisánye utúpáále twáake*
1.RM.see 2.all   2.ANT.be_asleep so 1.tie.SUBJ   13.gourds 13.3S.POSS
'he saw all were asleep, so then he tied together his three small gourds

uné nee tífugatile   *imishúúka yáá   tááta   n'úmaáyi*
me 1S   FUT.1S.take_care_of.FUT 4.spirits 4.LNK 1a.father and-1a.mother
as for me, I will take charge of the spirits of father and mother'

In the preceding sentences, one might expect to find *iisila yaake*'his way'
indexed on the verb because it is definite. It is unclear why it is not, if object
agreement is determined by definiteness.

An unusual aspect of object marking in Chindali is that pronominal use of
the marking is rarely found. Once an object has been identified, it typically is
not marked again where it is understood from context. Consequently, transitive verbs typically do not appear with an overtly expressed object.

tukweega amaléshi tukufúbika
1P.CO.take 6.millet 1P.CO.soak
'we take millet [and] we soak [it]'

bámu bakweega ingáambo bakufuundika mukalíbo ínga bakwéésa;
palá báásha bámu bakumyáándaga bámu bakukweesa múumbuno

'some take the tobacco, put [it] in a pipe, and smoke [it];
when they have ground [it], some lick [it], some smoke [it] through the
nose'

tukapakalaga íny'eemba; tukashaanga palwáala poo tusuungulúshe
páchooto poo tubíike múkasupa

'we used to apply *nyemba* on the skin; we used to grind [it] on a grinding
stone, then make [it] liquid over a fire, then put [it] in a small bottle'

ichipóonde bakoonganya imbatáata n'amálíma. Bakupíiya, poo liingá
fyáápya bakupoondanyán'umútiimgo. Palá baapóonda poo bakulábula
bakúlya.

'for *chiponde* they mix potatoes and beans; they cook [them], then when
they are done, they mash [them] with a wooden spoon; when they have
mashed [them], then they serve [them] and eat [them]'

161

❖ Coordination

• Nominal coordination

Simple coordination of nouns, including locative and infinitival forms, is achieved with the use of the particle *na* (cliticized as *n-* before vowel-initial words). Included in this are both the verbal nouns (i.e., infinitives) of class 15 and locative nouns.

> *akabá n'ábaana bábili, umulumyáana n'umúliindu*
> 'she had two children, a boy and a girl'

> *bakugula ingúúmbe n'imbáale*
> 'they buy a clay pot and crockery'

> *pámúúsi na pábushiku* 'during the day and at night'

> *ichíisu chikaanda ukúuma n'ukukema ingémyeeka*
> 'the land began to dry up and to crack'

Linking of nouns as subjects, however, is realized in one of three ways: through symmetric coordination, through asymmetric coordination, or through use of a comitative construction.

• Symmetric coordination

In symmetric coordination, the nouns are linked, as in the manner noted above, by the particle *na*. The subject agreement prefix on the verb is the appropriate third-person plural form if both nouns are of the same singular class, but class 8 *fi-*, if they are from different classes.

> *abasúkwa n'abáándali bakwiikala pamúpééne*
> 2.Sukwa and-2.Ndali 2.CO.live
> 'the Sukwa and Ndali peoples live together'

> *popáapo ngumany'á n'úmuusugu ichíindali n'ichisúkwa figelííle*
> 7.Ndali   and-7.Sukwa 8.be_similar.CMPL
> 'that's why, I know, even today, Chindali and Chisukwa are similar'

> *umuny'amáata n'umúliindu bakwaandá táashi bapulíkane íshaa*
> 1.young_man   and.woman   2.CO.begin

>   *lugáno béene*

> 'a young man and woman start first by agreeing about
> love on their own'

> *ámatone n'íisugu   fikakupuká   fyóoshi*
> 6.bananas and-10.sugu 8.RM.spill_out 8.all
> 'the bananas and *isugu* spilled out, all [of them]'

> *imbáale n'amapóoto fili   muchíingasha*
> 10.plates and.6.pots   8.be 18.7.kitchen
> 'the plates and pots are in the kitchen'

162

• Asymmetric coordination

Asymmetric coordination occurs when one of the subject nominals is, semantically, a pronominal. The pronominal is not expressed, but understood through the subject prefix on the verb, which is invariably plural. The co-ordinated noun itself occurs with the particle *na*, but follows the verb instead of preceding it. Hence, 'I' is expressed through affixation of the subject prefix *tu-* 'we'.

*pabúyo bwóo uné ngiimáápo, **tu-ka-palaman-á**   n'úmukolo   yúmo yóo*
                                   1P-RM-be_next_to-F and-1.woman

   íchikolo cháake akabá wii Náambene

'at the place where I was standing, we were next to each other—I and a certain woman whose surname was Nambene'

***tu-kaa-lí tu-ku-yugiisany-á** n'uNáambene abáandu bakaanda pakwíika*
1P-PRS-be 1P-CO-talk.REC-F and-1a.Nambene
'as we were still talking to each other—Nambene and I—people started to get off [the plane]'

*palá nááti nííkale pánu táa **tu-pulíkan-e** n'úmukulu wáangu   úyu*
                              NEG 1P-agree-SUBJ and-1.brother 1.1S.POSS 1.this
'if I decide to stay here we—this brother of mine and I—will not get along'

tu-ka-talikilan-á   ná-we
1P-RM-be_far_apart-F and-3S
'we—he and I—were far apart [physically]'

***mu-ku-buuk-á ná-we** kuny'úumba yaa múliindu*
2P-CO-go-F   and-3S
'you [pl]—you [sg] and he—go to the house of the young woman'

***mu-kw-iikal-a** pakatéefu n'umúny'ááko yóo ulí nágwe*
2P-CO-sit-F   and-1.friend
'you [PL]—you [SG] and your friend whom you [sg] are with [him]—sit on a mat'

*akati isóopo **shitákabááko**   n'ámafuta*
      5.soap 10.NEG.RM.be.17 and-6.oil
'he said there was no soap and oil [=lotion] there'

ákiimbile káake fi-paambanité léka n'ubúsaamba pámu n'ichiméle
12.manner   8-differ-CMPL   14.busamba   7.chemele
'its manner of performance they differ a lot from each other, [*akapote*] with *busamba* or with *chimele*'

163

• Comitative

The comitative construction resembles closely the asymmetric construction. It differs in that a singular subject may occur and, if so, it is marked with a singular subject prefix on the verb.

> *a-ku-bweel-á kwaábo n'umúfuusha*
> 1-CO-return-F   with-1.marriage_repreentative
> 'he returns to their [= his and the rep's] place with his marriage
> representative'

> *tishiku ílyaa níngeelo uChúungu akakoolela ulukomáano ukuti*
> *a-komáan-e n'abáandu   báake*
> 1-meet-SUBJ with-2.people
>
> 'the next day Chungu announced a meeting so that he could
> meet with his people'

> *akutí aa.lamúúngan.a n'ábo bwiisábwíísa, akúfuma*
>   1.ANT-greet-F   with-3P
> 'after she has exchanged greetings with them nicely, she goes out'

> *bakamusala ukuti wee íise aamul-án-ag-e   n'ábo*
>   1.ANT.answer-REC-IMPF-F with-3P
> 'they chose her so that she would come discuss together with them'

> *a-ka-tuulan-ag-á   n'aboowáámwabo*
> 1-RM-help-REC-IMPF-F with-1a.younger_brother
> 'he collaborated with his younger brothers'

• Verbal coordination

Coordination of verb phrases is marked by the particle *na* followed by the second verb in its nominal [infinitival] form. In VP coordination, not only are the subjects identical, but typically the objects are as well; or, the coordinated actions may be semantically similar.

> *bakasekesááshé n'ukusemeendeshááshe ubúfu*
> 'they just ground *and* winnowed flour'

> *bakumubiika mumbokóosi n'ukumushíila*
> 'they put him in a coffin *and* bury him'

> *bakapiiya ífyaakúlya n'ukweenga ubwáalwa bwaa maléshi*
> 'they cooked food *and* brewed millet beer'

• Clausal coordination

 • Asyndetic coordination

Asyndetic coordination involves simple juxtaposition of the linked clauses with no overt marking of coordination.

164

tukweega ifíloómbe tukubiika mukáti mukásefulila
'we take some maize [and] we put [it] inside a small pot'

akapaangulá akaaga mukáti maseléeti géene gakushuungúlila
'he broke [it] apart [and] found inside just flat things going around'

iiny'áma liingá sháápya báálya, bámu bakwaanda pakwiimba ubúsaamba
'when the meat is cooked [and] they have eaten, some start to perform the *busamba* dance'

akiikifyá mpáka akayá íímama
'she endured until she went [and] she hid'

• Sequential or supplementive coordination

If two clauses are temporally sequential, they are coordinated by *ínga*. The same particle is used when the second clause adds supplemental information to the first clause.

bámu bakweega ingáambo bakufuundika mukalíbo ínga bakwéésa
'some take the tobacco, put [it] in a pipe, *and then* smoke [it]'

poo palá lúmo gwéega indóófani ínga gwéega akapúúsa kaa ny'áma gwáálya, gwée poo fikúnoga
'so, if you take a potato *and then* you take a piece of meat [and] eat [them], mmmm, it tastes so good'

pala úmweeshi gwaasómoka ínga guseendamíte báti bwoo gulí n'ifisékéma
'if a new moon has appeared *and in additon* it was slanted, they say that it [moon] had brought malaria'

• Serial coordination

In serial coordination, each clause manifests agreement with the same subject. In addition, each clause after the initial one is expressed in the subjunctive form of the verb, hence, it occurs with final *-e*.

lúmo bakeega ubugáli babíike kwíifiga.
'sometimes they would take *bugali* [and] they would put [it] on a hearthstone'

bóoshi pákaaya bakiitisanyá basáyage ukuti abashúúka bahóboke
'all in the village would call to each other [and] they would give a sacrifice so that the spirits would be happy'

yúmo umukúumbi akwiisá alíbuule íifumu ilyoosóongo
'some digger comes [and] tells the head chief'

umugáanga akuyá ashíingule n'ilóóngwi
'the medicineman goes [and] smears [it] with mud'

165

akubuuká áyiikálage kuchípataala
'she goes [*and*] stays at the hospital'

abáandu bakakiindagá báye bíímame kumábwe gála gála
'people used to run away [*and*] go [*and*] hide in those rocks'

• Contrastive coordination

A contrast between coordinated clauses is indicated by *lóole* 'but'.

akagela ukuséenga, lóole akapóótwa
'he tried to build [it], but he failed'

úmukolo yúmo aasófya úmwaana, lóole abáandu batákabá náfyo n'imbóombo
'a certain woman had lost a child, but people didn't care'

umúliindu akabá chínuunu, lóole akabá mwíisa
'the girl was mute, but she was beautiful'

tukukuumbáashe ichibwíina, lóole chitákuba chítalí ngááni
'we just dig a pit, but it is not a very deep one'

• Alternative coordination

Alternative coordination is indicated in several ways. The most common form is *pámu* 'or', which may be used for simple nouns, infinitival phrases, or clauses.

póopo tukwiimbaga ichiméle pámu ubúsaamba
'that's when we perform the ichimele or ubusaamba dances'

bataangííkala pamupáando pámu pachitéengu
'they cannot sit on a chair or on a stool'

lúmo biitilanité beenébééne pakúlima pámu pakubega amaléshi
'sometimes they invited each other to cultivate or to harvest millet'

umúundu ali wéeshï yúuyo afwiile pangóosi pámu iikuungíte...
'each person who dies in an accident or hangs himself...'

shikabonáá shikutyéémula pámu shikukosómola ...
'when they [cattle] coughed or sneezed...'

If used before each coordinated word, *pámu* expresses the equivalent of 'either...or'. Note that *pámu* also has the sense of 'perhaps', which is undoubtedly related to its use as an alternative coordinator.

balí n'ábaana, pámu bábili pámu bátatu
'they have children, either two or three'

166

A second means of indicating 'either...or' alternatives is to place the form *napóo* before each constituent.

> *tukaseengaga utushéenga **napóo** twaa masééngo **napóo** twaa maláashi*
> 'we used to build huts either of wood or of bamboo'

A third means of introducing alternative possibilities is through use of *káli* before each constituent. This is equivalent to 'whether X or Y'.

> ***káli** múkolo **káli** múliisha tukwoongaanááshe pakumogá pamúpééne twéeshi*
> '*whether* it's a woman *or* a man, we all just mix together when dancing'

Finally, the form *ólo* is a recent borrowing from English that may be supplanting the traditional form *pámu*.

> *muJulai **ólo** Ógasti*
> 'in July or August'

> *...pala indaláma yaa sóopo **ólo** ímbééya yaatámya*
> '...when money for soap or salt is a problem'

> *néege chíliku íchaakuti imbíiye **ólo** índye?*
> 'I should take which [food] such that I cook or I eat?'

❖ **Gerundive phrases with *kuu-***

The proclitic *kúu=* is attached to simple infinitival forms following a verb in the indicative or presumptive moods. This clitic creates what can be considered to be a gerundive phrase, giving the sense of 'definitely and absolutely', often translated as 'just'. Compare this with post-final *-she* 'just' (in the sense of 'merely').

> *uungáaga uliilé lúkulu, kupootwá n'ukwéenda **kúu=kw-iikal-áá-she** pamúkulúlu, kwaagulá **kúu=kw-aagula** ngáti ubiníte, ngímba háaga.*

> 'you may find that you eat too much, you fail even to walk, *absolutely* just sitting on the verandah, you yawn, *just* yawning like you are sick, yet [you are] not'

> *tí-b-aa-gúl-ag-e **kúu=kwáágula*** 'they will be yawning, just yawning'

> *tíse alyáange **kúu=kú-lya*** 's/he will be eating, just eating'

❖ **Relative clauses**

Unlike many Bantu languages, Chindali does not differentiate subject and object relatives, using the same types of marking for each. Nevertheless, the two are separated below to isolate the two for illustrative purposes.

Chindali has numerous relative pronouns (see pages 35-40). For purposes here only a few of the many possibilities are illustrated.

• Subject relatives

*abáliisha **báabo** boosoongosóongo **bóo** bakwiikala*
2.men 2.COP.2.REL 2.COP.REL 2.RM.stay

 kuny'úumba kulá n'umúfiimba

'men *who are* elders *are the ones who* stay at the house with the corpse'

*úmukolo **weyúuyo** akuya kúkaaya kaa múliisha*
1.woman 1.COP.1.1.COP 1.CO.go

'the woman *is the one who* goes to the home of the man'

*umúundu **yóo** akwiisa kuyugá náwe **wéeyo** akuya*
1.person 1.REL 1.CO.come INF.speak with.3S 1.COP.1.REL 1.CO.go

  kweegiwááko

'the person *who* manages to talk with her *is the one whom* she is going to marry

*bakukuumbaga ubwíina bwaa kumushiila umúundu **yúuyo***
  afwííle 1.person 1.COP.1.REL
  1.die.CMPL

'they dig a hole for burying the person *who is* dead'

*abáandu **bóo** bakakweela mukáti mundéege múla bakaanda*
2.people 2.REL 2.RM.ride inside in.9.plane 9.that 2.RM.begin

 pakwíika
 16.15.get_off

'people *who* were riding inside that plane began getting off'

*wéeshi **yóo** íisa pambúungo akubá n'úbwiigane bwaa*
1.anyone 1.REL 1.ANT.come LOC.9.funeral 1.CO.be with.14.pleasure 14.LNK

 kubiikáápo kámu
 15.put.LOC 12.something

'anyone *who* has come to the funeral has the pleasure of giving something'

*ábakolo aboosóongo **bóobo** bakubasubiishaanga abáfwiilwe*
2.women 2.elderly 2.COP.2.REL 2.CO.2.console 2.bereaved

 *muny'úumba **mwóo** umufíimba gugoníte*
 18.9.house 18.COP 3.corpse 3.lie.CMPL

'elder women *are the ones who* console the bereaved family
in the house *in which* the corpse is lying'

168

*akáfulufulu, íimbepo **yóo** yikushuungulílaga*
12.whirlwind 9.wind   9.REL 9.CO.go_in_circles
'whirlwind, a wind *that* goes in circles'

*ábaaná báába bakaya pachishíba **páapo***   *chítalí ngááni*
                                   16.7.pool   16.COP.16.REL 7.deep
'these children used to go to a pool *in which* it is very deep'

*akóókábwa **kóo**   kaawiilíile*   *múmiishi   kaafúbuka*
12.dog   12.that 12.ANT.fall.APP.CMPL in.6.water 12.ANT.come_out
'the puppy that fell into the water has come out'

- Object relatives

  - Primary Objects

  *palá waapúlika ipéenga kulekeesha **imbóombo** yóoshi **yóo**
     waabóómbaga*
  'when you hear the *ipenga* drum, you stop all work that you have
  been doing'

  ***úmweenda gúugo** aboosékulu bakakwéény'aga gukabaanga mwéélufu*
  'the cloth that our grandparents wore was white'

  ***ífyaakulyá fyóo** bakalyáanga fyofyóo bakapayaga ukufuma mútwaaya
     twáabo*
  'the food that they ate was that which they brought with them from
  their homes'

  *bakayibona **indéege yóo** bakayiliindilílaga*
  'they saw the plane that they were waiting for'

  ***ábaana bíitu báabo** tukuya pakupáapa táabátwaage utusuúmo
     naatúmo naatúmo utú nguliingaanya pánu*
  'our children who we are going to bear will find not one of these
  dances I am describing here'

  *aba**páapi báabo** ngayúgaga aáma biisíle*
  'the parents that I spoke about, well, they have come'

  - Locative objects

  ***ichipáanga chóo** kwiipuutáámwo* 'the church that you pray in'

169

❖ **Oblique clauses**

• Conditional clauses [dependence of one circumstance on another]

Adverbial clauses of condition may be introduced by either of two subordinating conjunctions, *liinga* or *pala*. Although these seem nearly synonymous and interchangeable to some speakers, there does appear to be a subtle distinction between them grounded in the suppostion underlying the proposition. The use of *liinga* often indicates that the proposition is a suppositional hypothesis, the use of *pala* that the proposition is assumed. This distinction is illustrated by the sets of examples that follow.

   i) *liinga úmwaana aapapíwa, tíse tusékele*
      'if [supposing] the child is born [alive], we will celebrate'

      pala úmwaana aapapíwa, tíse tusékele
      'when [assuming] the child is born [alive], we will celebrate'

   ii) *liinga uNjéeki abuukite kuChitípa, kookuti uAmbíle abuukite náwe*
      'if [supposing] Njeki went to Chitipa, it means that Ambile went with him' [no knowledge of whether the event occurred or not]

      pala uNjéeki abuukite kuChitípa, kookuti uAmbíle abuukite náwe
      'if [assuming] Njeki went to Chitipa, it means that Ambile went with him' [some grounds, e.g., secondhand report, that event occurred]

In cases where supposition is odd, *pala* is preferred. In contrast, when the outcome is in question, *liinga* is preferred.

      pala íisuba lyááfuma, tíiny'amuke ukubuuka kuChitípa
      'when [assuming] the sun comes up, I will set out to go to Chitipa'

      liingá íisuba lyááfuma,
      'if [supposing] the sun comes out ...' [e.g., if it's not cloudy]

      liingá akushílika, úmupe umuléembo úgu
      'if [supposing] s/he faints, give her/him this medicine'

      ?palá akushilika, ...
      'when [assuming] s/he faints,...'

Further support for the distinction is found in the following sentences, in which the use of *liinga* reflects supposition, the use of *pala* presupposition.

      uChúungu akaloonda ukumany'á liinga uLwáangwa aangába
         n'amáka gaakupela íifula
      'Chungu wanted to know if [supposing] Lwangwa had the power to create rain'

170

palá aangápela bwoo títúmany'e ukuti nalóoli uyú musúkwa
'if [assuming] he can create [it], that is when we will know that, truly, he is a Sukwa'

With both *pala* and *linga*, the main clause is often introduced by *poo* 'then'.

*pala umúliisha aasalíwa n'úmukolo pachilíingo, **poo** úmukolo aabáanga múkashi*
'if [assuming] a man had been chosen by a woman at the inheritance ceremony, then the woman became his wife'

*liinga umúundu yúuyo ááfwa áali mumogáayi, **poo** tukumukubila iing'óma*
'if [supposing] the person who has died was a dancer, then we beat drums for her/him

*liingá báámala pakushíila, **poo** usóongo waa chááliki chíla chíla akuluumbílila*
'if they have finished burying, then an elder of the church preaches'

If the event in the subordinate clause, i.e., in the protasis, is counterfactual, the same distinction between *pala* and *liinga* can be found.

palá ngabá n'indaláma, ngalí ngagula amálíma
'if [assuming] I had had money, I would have bought beans'

liingá ngaba mubiingí waany'áma, ngalí náátega ifipíingo pánu
'if [supposing] I were a hunter, I would set traps here'

• Hypothetical clauses of condition

Hypothetical situations are expressed through use of the dissociative tense marker *-ka-* in the protasis, which may be introduced either by *pala* or by *napóo*. The apodosis typically incorporates *ngalí* plus an indicative form of the verb.

*palá tukayimany'a iisíla, **ngalí** twaabúuka*
'if we knew the way, we would/could go'

*napóo tífula yikáwa, **ngalí** tukabúuka*
'even if it had rained, we would have gone'

The tense of the verb in the apodosis determines whether the hypothetical condition is interpreted as real or unreal. If the verb is marked with either *-ku-* or *-aa-*, the condition is interpreted as real. In contrast, if it is marked with *-ka-*, the condition is interpreted as unreal.

171

pala umwáana akaleka pakúlila,	*ngalí naagonáápo*
'if the child stopped crying,	I could sleep a bit' [now]
	ngalí ngagona
'if the child had stopped crying,	I could have slept'
palá ngabá n'indaláma,	*ngalí ngugula amálíma*
'if I had money,	I would buy beans' [generic]
	ngalí ngágula amálíma
'if I had had money,	I would have bought beans'

The modal auxiliary *ngalí* can be used not only in conditional sentences with *pala*, but also in non-conditional sentences expressing present possibility.

uNjéeki ngalí aakwááfwa,	*palá ukabáápo*
'Njeki could help you,	if he were here'
	lóole atákulóonda
	but he doesn't want to'

• Temporal clauses

Adverbial clauses of time may, like conditionals, be introduced by either *liinga* or *pala*. A third possibility is *páapo*. It remains unclear what determines the choice of one or the other.

palá naany'ámuka pángeélo, tímbuuke kuChitípa
'when I get up in the morning, I will go to Chitipa'

liinga akabalílo kaakwáana ákaakuti béégane, bakupaangana íishiku ílyaakuti umúliisha ákaye abóneke kúkaaya kwaa múliindu
'when the time has come for them to marry, they decide on the day that the young man should appear at the home of the young woman'

biiganité nganíngáani pakwiimbá palá úmweeshi gukúbala
'they like especially to sing when the moon is shining'

usékulu akabweelaga kumbóombo liinga íisuba lyííngila
'grandfather used to return home from work when the sun had set'

pala umúliindu iitikísha, umulumyáana akumupa indaláma yaa kugulila íchaakúlya, nganíngáani íinguku yíiyo bakumugogelá liingá akuya pakushííngila
'when the young woman has consented [to marriage], the man gives her money for buying food, especially a chicken, which they will kill [and cook] for him when he goes to propose marriage'

172

*úmwééne **páapo** akafwáanga akabaleka ábaana báake*
biingíbíingííshe chifúukwa úmwééne akeega ábakolo bátatu
'he, himself, when he died, he left behind many, many children
because he had married three women'

*akuya pakupiiyá péene **páapo** úmwaana áámala ímyeeshi mítatu*
'she starts to cook only when the child is three months old'

• Concessive clauses

Concessive clauses are introduced by either *poobúle* 'even though' or *napóo*
'even if'. They denote a contrast between the two circumstances expressed.
Thus, the event in the main clause is typically surprising or unexpected given
the nature of the event in the subordinate clause.

poobúle íifula yikúwa, tukubúuka
'even though it's raining, we are going' [now]

poobúle íifula yikawáanga, ngalí ngabúuka
'even though it was raining, I should have gone'

poobúle akabá n'ichilóonda chaa kulumiwá n'íinjoka, akiikifyá
'even though she had a snakebite, she made herself endure the pain'

napóo íifula yikúwa, tímbuuke
'even if it rains, I will go'

napóo íifula yikáwa, ngalí tukabúuka
'even if it had rained, we would have gone'

• Locative clauses

There are a variety of elements for indicating location. The most common are
built on *-oo* by the affixation of one of the locative class prefixes, *pa-, ku-, or
mu-*. At times, *pala* may also be used.

póo íilyooshi likufúuka bwoo umulílo gulíípo
'where smoke is coming out, it means fire is there'

*uné ngataangwaniká n'ukukeeta apá n'áapa ukuloondá **póo** pakiima*
úmaáyi yúla
'me, I was busy, looking here and there, looking for where she was
standing, that woman'

*útaáta akaashiimbula ukuti **kóo** tukusáámila imótóka nyíingííko léka*
'Father deceived me, saying where we were moving there were many
cars'

*ichikolélo chikunyoongaananyoongaana kúbukulu **kwóo** chikufweená*
kápaale
'the handle is crooked at the bigger end where it resembles a calabash'

173

mwóo akúgona mwíisa léka
'where it nests is very nice'

muny'úumba mwóo umúfiimba gugoníte
'in the house where the corpse is lying'

liingá bááfika pála pala ubúfwe búli, bakwaanda pakuliisha iing'óma
'when they arrive there where the death occurred, they begin to beat a
drum'

• Clauses of reason

There are two ways of introducing clauses of reason: through use of *páapo* or
use of *chifúukwa*.

> *usékulu twé baana tutamuméeny'e páapo twé biingi tupaapiwe kuno
> kuMaláawi*

'Grandfather, we children do not know him because many of us were
born here in Malawi'

> *abáandu bála bakagaandá léka páapo íchaakulyá choopé
> batákalyaanga íchaakufwáana*

'those people became very thin because food, too, they did not eat
enough'

> *bakaganáákó ngááni kumisúku chifúukwa chaakuti ámiishi gakaba
> mbwée*

'they liked Misuku a lot because water was plentiful'

> *úbwuumi bwáa kuno bukutamyá nalóoli chifúukwa kuno ingalimóoto
> shaa kwééndela naashímo*

'life here is very difficult because here [there are] no cars for transport
at all'

• Clauses of manner

The form *páapo* may also mark a manner clause.

> *akakeeta páase boo akupulikisha umpwáato úwaá bwe páapo
> likapyoolaga amakókwe ámakulu ámatali ágaa makamáka*

'he looked on the ground while he listened to the noise of the rock as
it broke large, tall, strong trees'

• Clauses of comparison

Comparison is indicated by *ngáti* 'as if'.

> *aáma akiikalááshe akafwaasááshe ngáti aliipó n'umúliisha*
'well, she was just living there, she was just content, as if she were there
with a man'

174

bakakuumbaga ubwíina **ngáti** *wii zyéenje poo nóo kufwogoombola*
   kuumbáfu
'they used to dig the hole [grave] as if for a latrine, without making an
opening in the side'

• Clauses of purpose

Purpose clauses are introduceded by *ukuti* 'so that'. If a word for reason, e.g.,
ifúundo 'reason', is used, then the complementizer requires agreement and the
linker *-aa-*, hence *y-aa-kuti*.

   múúsiimbile **ukuti** *imbáliingaanyé bwíísa*
   'write me in order that I explain [them] to you well

   bakasuungila ífyaakulyá fíla fíla **ukuti** *fífike pakabalilo ákatali*
   'they preserve that food so that it may keep for a long time'

   ábakolo bakufugaga amagáli ámiingi **ukuti** *ichiluundílo chíicho*
   chiisíle chifwáane náfyo ífyaakúlya
   'women cook a lot of *magali* so that the crowd that has come should
have enough food'

   pámwaany'a akubiikáápo ichípóso **ukuti** *íifula many'é*
   yimútoony'elage palá agoníte
   'on top it [hammerkop] puts grass so that the rain will not drip on it
when it is sleeping'

   ifúundo yóo tukupímaga **yaakuti** *fiyáane ná chila ichikókwe*
   twaabíísaga
   'the reason why we measure is so that it should fit that piece of wood
we have been carving'

   ifúundo íingulu yóo bakaloondelaa ukuti úlwiiba luyáa mutúsakasa
   twáab yikabá **yaakuti** *ing'óombe shíla báti shilyáa na pábushiku*
   múla múla
   'the main reason why they wanted the grass to go into their huts was so
that the cattle would eat in there even at night'

• Clauses of result

Result clauses are introduced by *úlwaakuti*.

   umufúúngúla wáá nduuny'e gukakulaga **úlwaakuti** *abáandu*
   bakany'amusanyagááshe bátatu
   'a stalk of bananas used to grow so [large] that it had to be carried
by three people'

175

*bakaseembelelaga útuseke twaa kóofi mupáka túkule **úlwaakuti***
  twaapalámila pabukúshi
'they used to water the little coffee seeds until they grew so that they
came close to maturity'

❖ Agreement resolution

• Subjects

With plural subjects belonging to different noun classes, agreement
on the verb is resolved in one of two ways. The most common appears to be
through use of the default agreement marker *fi-*, regardless of what classes the
nouns belong to.

ichóongo chaá kalulu n'ukwiimba kwaa lusekélo fikashiindilagá		
7.noise	15.sing	8.RM.plug.IMPF

  n'ifyúufwo

'the noise of ululations and joyous singing even stopped up [deafened]
the ears'

ngímba ifígaamba n'ímishitu fikwaagibwá kwóoki		
8.mountains	4.forests 8.CO.find.PASS	

'the mountains and forests are found where?'

iibóga lyíitu tukalyaanga ífitugo n'íbiíndu	*fyóo n'uutwé*
8.yams and-5.yam_leaves	8.REL

  fi-ka-fweená mbatáata
  8-RM-resemble

'[as for] our *iboga*, we ate yam leaves and yams which, for us,
were like sweet potatoes'

pakabalílo kála kála imiséébo n'iisíláashe fi-tá-ka-b-áá-kwo	
4.roads and 9.paths	8-NEG-RM-be-F-17

'at that time roads and paths just did not exist there'

ákiimbile káake fi-paambanité léka n'ubúsaamba pámu n'ichiméle			
12.manner	8-differ-CMPL	14.busamba	7.chimele

'its manner of performance differs a lot from *busamba* or *chimele*'

A second resolution strategy, apparently less common than the first and not
accepted by all speakers, requires agreement of the verb with the closest noun.

ámatone n'íísúgu shóo uNáambene akany'ámula shi-ka-kupuk.á	
6.bananas 10.legume	10-RM-pour_out

  shóoshi
  10.all

'the bananas and *isugu* that Nambene was carrying poured out, all'

• Objects

Agreement resolution for object indexation follows the less common pattern for subjects. Whatever the classes of the two nouns might be, the verb is marked to agree only with the noun closest to it.

*akayá   aa-**mú**-laga   usékulu   n'úmaáma*
1.RM-go 1.ANT-1-bid_farewell_to 1a.grandfather and-1a.grandmother
'he went and bid farewell to grandfather and grandmother'

*a-ku-**li**-loonda **íikasu**   n'umúkóolo   wáake*
1-CO-5-look_for 5.digging_hoe and-3.planting_hoe 3.3S.POSS
'he is looking for his digging hoe and planting hoe'

*a-ku-**gu**-loonda **umúkóolo**   n'íikasu   lyáake*
1-CO-3-look_for 3.planting_hoe and-5.digging_hoe 5.3S.POSS
'he is looking for his digging hoe and planting hoe'

Object nouns, however, may be right dislocated, in which case object marking on the verb exhibits a pronominal function. When nouns are of the same class, the approriate plural marker for the class is used; if they are from different classes, -*fi*- is used.

*ba-ku-**ba**-p-a ulusáko ukuti báyugéépo   shímo, ábaalúko*
2-CO-2-give-F 11.chance so_that 2.say-SUBJ-bit 10.some 2.relative

    n'umuny'afyáale
    and.1.head_chief

'they give them a chance to say something, the relatives and the head chief'

*mwoo akaali ukuny'ámuka akayá aa-**bá**-laga,   usékulu*
    n'úmaáma   1.ANT-2-bid_farewell 1.grandfather
    1.grandmother

'before he had yet set off, he went [and] bid them farewell, grandfather and grandmother'

*a-ku-**fi**-lóonda, íikasu   n'umúkoólo*
1-CO-8-look_for 5.digging_hoe and-3.planting_hoe
'he's looking for them, the digging hoe and the planting hoe'

❖ **Locatives as subjects**

Locative noun phrases may occur as syntactic subjects. The verb takes the appropriate locative agreement prefix. The logical semantic subject, such as *iinjoka* 'snake', occurs following the verb and cannot be omitted. Most cases of locative subjects occur with the verb 'be', either with defective -*li* or *uku.ba*.

*pamuséébo ápo pa-fwiiliile íinjoka poo pa-ku-nuungá léka paakuti
    yibolíte*

'on the road there [there] died a snake which smells bad because it is
rotten'

pásiíla ápo pa-li ubukwáati 'nearby up there there is a wedding'

...ukuti páapo bakuséenga pá-b-e págolofu
'...so that where they were building would be flat'

kuMisúku ku-li ifígaamba léka 'in Misuku there are lots of hills'

muny'úumba mu-li abagéni 'in the house there are visitors'

mwóo bakalíma mu-ka-báá-mwo ichípóso chímo chíicho tukuti úlwiiba
'where they were farming there was a certain grass that we call *ulwiba*'

*múmushitu waa Mugése mu-ka-báá-mwo ichishíba chíicho chikaba
    páasi ngááni*
'in the forest of Mugese was a pool of water that was very deep'

❖ Existential constructions

Existential constructions are formed with the verb 'be', either *-li* or *-ba*, or *-ti*
'say'. There are three different types of construction, differing in how agreement is marked on the verb. All incorporate a locative element.

• "Dummy" agreement prefix *ku-*

In indicative constructions, all verbs require an agreement prefix. When there
is no noun to determine agreement, as in simple existential constructions, the
"dummy" locative prefix *ku-* is affixed.

ku-li íimbepo 'it's windy' [= there is wind]

pála aáma ku-ku-ba ífyaakúlya lúmo kwaagá babagogiile íinguku
'well, when there is food, perhaps you [APO] find they kill a chicken
for you [PL]'

ku-ka-tíí-she mwetú 'there just flashed lightning'

ku-k-aand-á n'ukupulikwa útululu n'ukwiimbá kwaa báandu
'there began even to be heard ululations and the singing of people'

• Sans nominal agreement: LOC – T/Ten – BE – LOC

In more complex existential constructions, there are both initial and final locative affixes attached to the verb 'be'. Any of the three locative class prefixes
may occur, typically the same class in both positions. However, two different
classes may also occur.

pa-lii-po akáfwiilile kaa múundu kakukiindanakíindana
'there are different ways a person dies'

178

ku-lii-pó kúmo ukúfwa kwaakuti umúundu bamulogíte
'there is a certain way of dying such that a person is bewitched'

mu-lii-mwó shímo ímbaanga shíisho shikakuukáápo
'there are some caves that are very scary'

ku-tá-ka-báá-ko ichigáayo naachímo naachímo muMisúku
'there was no grinding mill at all in Misuku' [remote past]

palá baashíila, ku-ku-báá-kwo imbóombo yaa chiipúuto n'ukusopa
ífyaabúpe

'when they have buried [the corpse], there remains the task of prayers
and offering of gifts'

pa-ku-báá-kwo ukubafuunda abáandu bábili ába múbuumi bwáabo
ubúpya
'there is advising [of] these two people about their new life'

• With nominal agreement: **AGR** – T/Ten – **BE** – **LOC**

In the third type of existential construction, the noun functions as the syntactic
subject determining agreement on the verb, but typically follows the verb. A
locative enclitic—derived from any of the three locative classes—occurs in
final position on the verb.

lu-lii-po ululagílo úlukafú ngááni
11-be-16 11.rule   11.hard
'there is a very strict rule'

ba-lii-pó sóóna abóótááta aboosóongo
2-be-16   2.men   2.elderly
'there are also elderly men'

soóna akukeetesha ukuti abany'afyáale n'abáandu ubúpulikane
  bu-líí-po   11.unity
  11-be-16

'also he makes sure that [between] the chiefs and the people unity
exists'

li-ku-báá-po íishiku líilyo bóoshi ábaa pámbuumba yáabo
5-CO.be-16   5.day   5.REL

  bakukomáana

'there is a day when all those in the(ir) extended family meet'

chi-lii-kó chímo ichíteengele bakuti koo kwaa Nakamúundu
7-be-17   7.certain 7.woods
'there is a certain woods which they say is the home of Nakamundu'

179

shi-lii-kó shímo   únjoka   bakuti abóóchipili
10-be-17   10.some 10.snakes
'there are some snakes they call puff-adders

fi-lii-kó fímo   ifiyúni bakutukaanila pakúlya
8-be-17   8.some 8.birds
'there are some birds they forbid us to eat'

❖ Equational constructions

Equational sentences assert that two nominal referents are equivalent. In Chindali, one of the referents appears as the topic of the sentence, the other as the syntactic subject of the verb 'be'. The subject follows the verb but determines agreement.

báti ifiyúníí fíífyo   shi-ku-bá ndéege shaa   balóshi
2.say 8.bird   8.8.those 10-CO.be   10.plane 10.LNK   2.witch
'they say those birds, they are planes of witches'

ukunuusha íchaakúlya ka-táa   kasúmo   kíisa   kukwíitu
                            12-NEG.be 12.custom 12.good
'smelling food [it] is not a good habit in our place'

❖ Ellipsis

There are few examples of ellipsis. Two cases illustrate the omission of the verb in the first example, of a noun in the second. Somewhat surprisingly, it is the first noun that is omitted in the second case, so that the intended reading is 'mix bananas with beans'.

*bámu bakukomaga útukono, bámu utulúúlu, poo kwaagá n'úlwiimbo
lwááshila*

'some clap [beat] hands, some _____ ululations, then you find the song is finished'

*shímo bakoonganya iiny'áma n'índuuny'e; shímo bakoonganyá
n'amálíma*

'in some, they mix meat with bananas; in some, they mix _____ with beans'

180

PART 9

INVARIABLE FORMS

❖ Conjuncts

Conjunct elements indicate the kind of connection between what is currently being said and what has been said previously in the discourse event.

tááshi	'first'
lóole	'however, but'
napáapo	'even if'
poo	'and then, so then'
poobúle	'even though, although'
póope	'even so'
soóna	'also, too'
soóna kwóope	'furthermore'
búno búno	'consequently'
pabumalílo	'finally'

❖ Discourse particles

Discourse markers function in the context of an extended interaction to mark the functional relationship of one clause or sentence to another.

aáma 'well'

introduces a remark: *abapáapi báabo ingayúgaga aáma biisíle* 'the parents that I spoke about, well, they have come'

expresses resigned assent: *aáma naapúlika, lóole aboowíise naabámu* 'well, I understand, but [her] fathers are not available'

emphasizes a point: *aáma mwomúumwo* 'indeed, it is the case'

ápo 'there'

exclamation of completion: *ápo twáámala ipenéenga* 'there! we have finished the *ipenenga* drum'

ése 'well then'

expression of sufferance: *ése poo náálita* 'well, then, I'm tired'

namáanga 'you know'

namáanga ábééne bakaboombelaa amákweéla ngáti poo yáába ngúbo

'you know, they, in fact, used animal skins as though they were cloth'

183

❖ Evidentials

Chindali speakers have the option of indicating the source of the knowledge expressed in a proposition—either the self or the other—combined with the mode of knowing—inference or secondhand report. In both cases, the speaker effectively reduces his or her responsibility for the accuracy or truth of the assertion.

fweení 'it seems'

> *fweení atákuloonda ukuti áambe indaláma shóoshí shííshi*
> 'it seems he does not want to give me all of that money'

> *fweení baliilé kále* 'it seems they have eaten already'

> *lóole kumáshu góo gaaloondiwáanga fweení náámala góoshi*
> 'but as to discussion, it seems I have finished all that is needed'

> *akápaango kaa báándali liingá tuuti tukokotéshe kóoshi*
> *fweení tíse túmale amapéépála ámiingi léka*
> 'if we were to tell in detail the whole story of the Ndali people,
> it seems we would have to use a lot of paper'

báti 'they say; it is said'

> *báti abalóshi balí n'akabíni léka* 'they say witches are very jealous'

> *pala íifula yikuwa ububíibi báti bakayaa pakwiipuuta mukayúumba*
> *kála kála*

> 'if it's raining badly, it is said they used to go to pray in that hut'

❖ Interjections

• Expressions of negation

i'i 'no'

aáwe 'no'

nashíku 'not at all'

> *tutákwiimba ámashiku góoshi ágaa mbúungo aáwe náshiku*
> 'we do not perform on all days of the funeral, no, not at all'

háaga [expression of strong negation]

> *poo uné ndákakaaná háaga*
> 'so, me, I didn't refuse, not in the least'

• Expressions of dissatisfaction

aasé [exclamation of blame or anger]

> *aasé kupíika* 'fool, you are lying!'

184

asée [exclamation of disgust]

> *asée ndaangalíila múno, muny'alité léka*
> 'yech, I can't eat in here; it's too dirty'

báasi [expression of finality]

> *báasi íny'eéga yaashíita* "that's it', the marriage is off'

éena 'yes (is that so?)' [when one is not satisfied with an answer]

- Expression of uncertainty

ndíishi 'I don't know'

> *aáma ndíishi akayúni aáma kalíípo kakusebasebá pánu panú ndíishi*
>
> 'well, I don't know, a bird [unmarried girl], well, is here, picking up around here, I don't know'

- Expressions of affirmation

iínga 'yes'

isága 'expression of welcome'

éena response to *isága*

enáala [exclamation of happiness]

> *enáala twaagáaga ámiishi* 'hey heeey, we have found water!'

búle [expression of encouragement]

> *búle maáyi utákuguláápo?*
> 'how about it, ma'am, are you not going to buy some?'

- Miscellaneous expressions

> ***aandági*** 'sorry' [expression of condolence]
>
> ***aléege*** 'here you are' [when handing someone something]

APPENDICES

APPENDIX A

VERB REFERENCE TEMPLATES

The reference templates illustrate the positions of various grammatical elements that occur as affixes on the verb. Items in bold are obligatory, items in plain text, optional.

❖ INDICATIVE MOOD

SP – NEG – **T/Ten** – OM– **BASE** – ASP – Vox – ASP – **F** – ASP = PoF

    -tá-   *-ku-*   *-ag-* *-a*

        -aa-   *-it-*   *-e*

        -ka-

                                                   -aa

        -nga-

❖ NON-INDICATIVE MOODS

  • PRESUMPTIVE [≈ FUTURE]

    tí – NEG – *se* **SP** – T – OM – **BASE** – Vox – ASP – *e* – ASP = PoF

      -a-   *-ka-*   *-ag-*   *-aa*

  • SUBJUNCTIVE

    NEG **SP** – T – OM – **BASE** – Vox – ASP – *e* = PoF

    many'é   *-ka-*   *-ag-*

  • EXHORTATIVE

    sáá **SP** – OM – **BASE** – ASP – *e*

                   -ag-

  • IMPERATIVE

    NEG OM – **BASE** – ASP – **F** = PoF

    kóoma   *-ag-* *-a*

                       -e

APPENDIX B

PARADIGM OF THE VERB *UKU.LIMA* 'cultivate; hoe'

The following list illustrates many, but not all, of the possible forms of the common activity verb *uku.lima* 'cultivate; hoe'. The divisions reflect the general organization of the Tense/Aspect system of the language.

Affirmative constructions

Coincident	*bakulima ifíloómbe*	'they cultivate maize'
		'they are hoeing the maize'
		'they have been hoeing the maize'
	bakufílima	'they cultivate it'
		'they are hoeing it'
	bali pakulima ifíloómbe	'they are hoeing the maize'
	bakaalí bákulima ifíloómbe	'they are still hoeing the maize'
	batákulimá táashi	'they are not hoeing yet'
Simple anterior	*báálima ifíloómbe*	'they have [just] hoed the maize'
	baafílima	'they have [just] hoed it'
	baalímaga	'they were hoeing'
		'they had been hoeing'
	báali pakúlima	'they were hoeing'
	bakáali bákufilima	'they were still hoeing it'
	báanda pakúlima	'they have begun hoeing'
	báaleka pakúlima	'they have stopped hoeing'
	báámala pakúlima	'they have finished hoeing'
	baalímagáashe	'they kept hoeing'
Current completive	*balimíte ifíloómbe*	'they hoed the maize'
	bafilimíte	'they hoed it'
Anterior completive	*baalimite ifíloómbe*	'they hoed the maize'
	baafilímite	'they hoed it'
	báándite pakúlima	'they began hoeing'
	baalékite pakúlima	'they stopped hoeing'
	baamálite pakúlima	'they finished hoeing'

190

Remote past	*bakalima ifíloómbe*	'they cultivated maize'
	bakafílima	'they cultivated it'
	bakafilímaga	'they were cultivating it' 'they used to cultivate it'
	bakaba pakúlima	'they were hoeing'
	bakabá bakaalí bákulima	'they were still hoeing'
	bakaanda pakufílima	'they began hoeing it'
	bakalimagááshe	'they kept hoeing'
	bakaleka pakúlima	'they stopped hoeing'
	bakamala pakúlima	'they finished hoeing'
Potential	*baangálima ifíloómbe*	'they can/could hoe the maize'
	baangafílima	'they can/could hoe it'
Presumptive [futures]	*tibálime ifíloómbe*	'they will hoe the maize'
	tíbáye pakúlima	'they will go hoe'
	tíbábe pakúlima	'they will be hoeing'
	tíbábe bakaalí bákulima	'they will still be hoeing'
	tíse bálime ifíloómbe	'they will hoe the maize'
	tíse báye pakúlima	'they will go hoe'
	tíse bábe pakúlima	'they will be hoeing'
	tíse bábe bakaalí bákulima	'they will still be hoeing'
Imperative	*lima ifíloómbe*	'hoe the maize'
	filíme	'hoe it'
	límaga	'hoe'
	filimáge	'hoe it'
	kalime ifíloómbe	'go hoe the maize'
	kafilíme	'go hoe it'
Subjunctive	*bálime ifíloómbe*	'they should hoe the maize' 'let them hoe the maize'
	bafílime	'they should hoe it' 'let them hoe it'

Negative constructions

Coincident	*batakulima ifíloómbe*	'they do not cultivate maize' 'they are not hoeing the maize' 'they have not been hoeing the maize'
	batákufílima	'they do not cultivate it' 'they are not hoeing it'
	batáa pakulima ifíloómbe	'they are not hoeing the maize'
	batákulimá tááshi	'they are not hoeing yet'
Simple anterior	*batáálima ifíloómbe*	'they have not [just] hoed the maize'
	bataafílima	'they have not [just] hoed it'
	bataalímaga	'they were not hoeing' 'they had not been hoeing'
	bataafilímagá tááshi	'they were not yet hoeing it'
	batáanda pakúlima	'they have not begun to hoe'
	batááleka pakúlima	'they have not stopped hoeing'
	batáámala pakúlima	'they have not finished hoeing'
Current completive	*batalimíte ifíloómbe*	'they did not hoe the maize'
	batafilimíte	'they did not hoe [= grow] it'
Anterior completive	*bataalímite ifíloómbe*	'they did not hoe the maize'
	bataafilímite	'they did not hoe it'
	batáándite pakúlima	'they did not begin to hoe'
	bataalékite pakúlima	'they did not stop hoeing'
	bataamálite pakúlima	'they did not finish hoeing'
Remote past	*batákalima ifíloómbe*	'they did not cultivate maize'
	batákafílima	'they did not cultivate it'
	batákafilímaga	'they were not cultivating it' 'they did not use to cultivate it'
	batákaba pakúlima	'they were not hoeing'
	batákalimagá tááshi	'they were not yet hoeing'
	batákaanda pakufílima	'they did not begin hoeing it'
	batákaleka pakúlima	'they did not stop hoeing'
	batákamala pakúlima	'they did not finish hoeing'

Potential	*bataangálima ifíloómbe*	'they can/could not hoe the maize'
	bataangafílima	'they can/could not cultivate it'
Presumptive [futures]	*táabálime ifíloómbe*	'they will not hoe the maize'
	táabafílime	'they will not hoe it'
	táabáye pakúlima	'they will not go hoe'
	táabábe pakúlima	'they will not be hoeing'
	táase bálime ifíloómbe	'they will not hoe the maize'
	táase bálime	'they will not hoe'
	táase báye pakúlima	'they will not go hoe'
	táase bábe pakúlima	'they will be hoeing'
Imperative	*kóóma ukulima ifíloómbe*	'don't hoe the maize'
	kóóma ukufílima	'don't hoe it'
Subjunctive	*many'é bálime ifíloómbe*	'they should hoe the maize' 'don't let them hoe the maize'
	many'é bafílime	'they should hoe it' 'don't let them hoe it'
	many'é bálime	'they shouldn't hoe' 'don't let them hoe'

REFERENCES

Bastin, Yvonne. 1978. "Les langues bantoues." In D. Barreteau (ed.), *Inventaire des Études Linguistiques*. Paris: Conseil International de la langue Française. Pp. 123-185.

Botne, Robert. 2003. "Dissociation in tense, realis, and location in Chindali verbs." *Anthropological Linguistics* 45, 4: 390-412.

Botne, Robert. 2006. "Motion, time, and tense: On the grammaticization of *COME* and *GO* to future markers in Bantu." *Studies in African Linguistics* 35, 2: 127-188.

Botne, Robert and Tiffany L. Kershner. To appear 2008. "Tense and cognitive space: On the organization of tense/aspect in Bantu languages. *Cognitive Linguistics* 19,3.

Gordon, Raymond G., Jr. (ed.). 2005. *Ethnologue: Languages of the World* (15th ed.). Dallas, Texas: SIL International.

Guthrie, Malcolm. 1967-70. *Comparative Bantu* (4 vols.). Farnborugh, England: Gregg Press.

Kershner, Tiffany L. 2001. "Imperfectivity in Chisukwa." In R. Botne and R. Vondrasek (eds.), *Explorations in African Linguistics: From Lamnso' to Sesotho* (Working Papers in Linguistics 3), IULC: Bloomington, IN. Pp. 37-52.

Kershner, Tiffany L. 2002. The verb in Chisukwa: Aspect, tense, and time. Ph.d. dissertation, Indiana University.

Kishindo, Pascal J. 1998. 'Diminution, augmentation and pejorativeness in Icindali: The semantics of classes 5/6, 3/4, 7/8 and 21.' *Journal of the Humanities* (Zomba, Malawi) 12: 44-55.

Newman, Paul. 1983. "The efferential (alias 'causative') in Hausa". In E. Wolff and H. Mayer-Bahlburg (eds.), *Studies in Chadic and Afroasiatic Linguistics*. Hamburg: H. Buske Verlag. Pp. 397-418.

Palmer, F. R. 2001. *Mood and Modality*. Cambridge, U.K.: Cambridge University Press.

Schadeberg, Thilo C. 2003. "Derivation". In D. Nurse and G. Philippson (eds.), *The Bantu Languages*. London and New York: Routledge. Pp. 71-89.

INDEX

W

www.ingramcontent.com/pod-product-compliance
Lightning Source LLC
Chambersburg PA
CBHW030305100426
42812CB00002B/576